To the memory of

my mother,

EVELYN BAUM CAHN,

and her brother

MORTON BAUM

Saints and Scamps

Saints and Scamps

Ethics in Academia

25th Anniversary Edition

Steven M. Cahn

ROWMAN & LITTLEFIELD PUBLISHERS, INC.
Lanham • Boulder • New York • Toronto • Plymouth, UK

Published by Rowman & Littlefield Publishers, Inc.
A wholly owned subsidiary of The Rowman & Littlefield Publishing Group, Inc.
4501 Forbes Boulevard, Suite 200, Lanham, Maryland 20706
http://www.rowmanlittlefield.com

Estover Road, Plymouth PL6 7PY, United Kingdom

British Library Cataloguing in Publication Information Available

Library of Congress Cataloging-in-Publication Data
Cahn, Steven M.
  Saints and scamps : ethics in academia / Steven M. Cahn.—25th anniversary
ed.
    p. cm.
  Includes bibliographical references and index.
  ISBN 978-1-4422-0566-6 (pbk. : alk. paper)—ISBN 978-1-4422-0567-3
(electronic)
  1. College teachers—Professional ethics. I. Title.
  LB1779.C34 2011
  174'.937812—dc22
                                        2010022478

∞ ™ The paper used in this publication meets the minimum requirements of
American National Standard for Information Sciences—Permanence of Paper
for Printed Library Materials, ANSI/NISO Z39.48-1992.

Printed in the United States of America

~

Contents

Foreword

I fell in love with this book in 1988 and have re-read it often. I always
view it as a brief retreat, as if returning to a friend who will give you
advice that you know is good and true. Over the years I have made it
my tradition to give this as a gift to new faculty, deans, and Trustees. I
am thrilled that it is now in the 25th anniversary edition. It will continue to grace the book collections of essential reading of my friends
and colleagues.

This is the book I wish I had had when I started my academic career. In a cogent manner, Dr. Cahn gets to the heart of our profession,
reviewing our major responsibilities to our students, colleagues and society. His experience as a provost and professor provide numerous real-
life challenges for those of us who toil in the fields of academia. The
simple truth is that we are engaged in a multifarious endeavor as we
balance competing needs and agendas. Dr. Cahn gently, but with firm
conviction, helps us deal with the complexity of our duties through a
review of the axioms of the profession and our ethical responsibilities.
Although I have never met Dr. Cahn, through this book he has been
a good mentor.

Thomas H. Powell, President Mount St. Mary's University

~

Preface to
the 25th Anniversary Edition

When Jon Sisk, my longtime editor at Rowman & Littlefield, reminded me that twenty-five years had passed since *Saints and Scamps* first appeared, I was surprised by how quickly the years had seemed to pass but pleased that the book was still in print.

The question I am most often asked about the work is whether it has led faculty members to devote greater attention to their moral obligations. I regret that even my limited hopes for improvement may have been overly optimistic. Most notably, the quality of graduate education at some highly regarded programs has taken a turn for the worse, as departments compete to achieve the highest possible national rankings.

This effort, unfortunately, has not involved strengthening curricula to ensure students' breadth of knowledge or developing courses in methods of teaching to enhance the pedagogical skills of future instructors. Instead, a favored approach is to persuade professors with high visibility to leave their home institutions and join others, offering them as incentives both the highest possible salaries and the lowest possible number of courses to teach. Obviously, few of today's leading scholars would be attracted by what used to be the standard teaching schedule at prestigious universities: one graduate and one undergraduate course each semester. Rather, attractive packages now include no undergraduate teaching and limited graduate teaching, perhaps no more than one course per semester, or even per year. The most appealing deals, however, go beyond these arrangements and involve an immediate sabbatical. In a case I know, a school's offer of a one-year release was topped by another school's two-year bid.

The departments in question were recruiting a highly regarded, although not great, moral philosopher. My advice to the losing department would be to consider adding to its masthead a far more prestigious name: Aristotle. Of course, he would not actually appear at the school but neither would the other celebrity professor. And both would do the same amount of teaching and advising: none at all. Furthermore, because national rankings depend not on whether professors are available but rather on whether their writings attract attention, Aristotle would be by far the stronger choice. Indeed, the following year the department could move further up the ranks by adding to its roster Kant. Maybe Nietzsche.

Granted, at some point even the most renowned professor is expected to teach at least one graduate course. Faced with this unwelcome task, however, a luminary can still maneuver by arranging to team-teach with a colleague, then invite guest speakers. The classroom can thus be turned into a professional colloquium, allowing the participants to pursue their research agendas under the guise of instruction.

As for comprehensive examinations, who these days wants to be bothered constructing or grading them? A common substitute is to require doctoral students to undertake qualifying papers, then suggest that preferred topics would be those within the research interests of the faculty. In that way, professors can concentrate on their own scholarly agendas.

As long as graduate students observe their professors viewing themselves as if they were pampered passengers on an academic cruise ship, the students are likely to imitate this selfish behavior. They will fail to understand that professors are supposed to be professionals, obligated to use their expertise to serve others.

Perhaps those who pay the bills for higher education will eventually realize that, when presidents, provosts, and deans point with pride to the high rankings their graduate departments enjoy, these administrators are not necessarily providing evidence that their students, whether graduate or undergraduate, are receiving a high-quality education. That goal can be achieved only if faculty members are willing to carry out conscientiously their extensive responsibilities.

What exactly are these? Providing an answer to that question led me to write *Saints and Scamps*.

In this new edition the text has been lightly edited. I have also appended five papers of mine, written after the book, that explore various aspects of academic ethics.

I wish to thank Jon Sisk for his continuing support; my brother, Professor Victor L. Cahn of the Department of English at Skidmore College, for his advice, editorial and otherwise; and my wife, Marilyn Ross, MD, for more than I can express in words.

This volume is dedicated to the memory of my mother, Evelyn Baum Cahn, a beloved high school English teacher, and her brother Morton Baum, who provided the administrative acumen and creative planning that led to the success of the New York City Center of Music and Drama, including the New York City Opera and the New York City Ballet. My mother and brother were inseparable, and their influence on me was incalculable.

~

Preface

Some years ago I was asked to deliver a lecture titled "Ethics in the Academic World." When I mentioned the topic to a faculty colleague, he remarked, "It'll be a short talk."

Remarkably little has been written about the obligations of a professor. Numerous books and articles have explored the rights of faculty members, but no corresponding literature examines their responsibilities. Yet surely professors, like physicians or attorneys, should be expected to adhere to high standards of professional conduct. We all know of careless doctors and dishonest lawyers, but these unscrupulous individuals have violated detailed codes of behavior, framed and ratified by their colleagues. What comparable code has been violated by an unscrupulous professor?

Students entering a college or university are entitled to presume that their instructors are dedicated professionals, committed to discharging their duties conscientiously. Too often, however, students are exposed to professors whose conduct is shameful. Virtually any undergraduate or graduate student can relate harrowing stories about tribulations suffered at the hands of irresponsible instructors. I have never forgotten my English composition teacher, who lectured incoherently, failed to appear for scheduled office hours, and awarded no grade higher than

C+. When one day in class he mentioned that another section of the same course had room for a few students, the announcement precipitated a stampede for the door.[1]

Such cases will surprise no one familiar with academic life. Indeed, to complain about such occurrences may strike some simply as a failure to appreciate the potential pedagogic value of idiosyncrasy. Whatever the charms of the stereotypical eccentric professor, however, they are no consolation to a student who has been neglected, misguided, or otherwise mistreated.

"Malpractice" is a term that has come to be associated primarily with physicians; yet, it applies to members of any profession who fail to exercise appropriate care in carrying out their duties. But what exactly are the duties of professors, and what are the appropriate standards of care? These are the questions I address in the following pages.

I recognize that students and administrators, as well as members of boards of trustees and alumni, from time to time confront ethical issues.[2] At the core of any college or university, however, is the faculty. Its informed evaluations lie at the heart of the educational process, and its critical role will be my focus.

A faculty that abuses authority is a disgrace, while one that lacks authority is a sham. But a college or university faculty that conscientiously exercises proper authority offers each student the opportunity to acquire that most precious gift, an educated mind. Loss of such an opportunity is always unfortunate but is especially painful when the cause is professional malfeasance.

CHAPTER ONE

~

The Professorial Life

In the early 1970s a book appeared with the provocative title *This Beats Working for a Living: The Dark Secrets of a College Professor*. The author's name was given only as "Professor X," although I later learned he headed the history department of a state university in the West. His skepticism about faculty members was epitomized in this blunt judgment: "I have met few professors whom I would hire to run a peanut stand, let alone be the guardian of wisdom and Western civilization."[1]

In this spirit I offer a brief sketch of a professor I once knew. He, too, will go unnamed, but in his day he was a respected scholar. He regularly canceled classes. At those he attended, he arrived late, and when he did arrive he was generally unprepared. He gave no examinations, so he would have none to correct. In each course he assigned one term paper, to which he gave a cursory reading. If he liked the few pages he read, he gave the paper an A. If he didn't like them, he gave the paper a B. Students who submitted no paper received a C. This grading system avoided most complaints, although on occasion a student who had received a B would protest that the grade should have been an A. The matter would always be settled quickly by the instructor's graciously consenting to alter the grade as requested. He left his mail unopened for weeks at a time, thus missing one deadline after another. He never attended a faculty meeting. He did attend departmental meetings, but whenever a critical vote was to be taken, he managed to be out of the room. When he was asked to fulfill an administrative task, his strategy was simple: he failed to appear at school and left the matter to the departmental secretary.

Surely this man was unethical. He held the honorable title of "professor" but systematically abused the responsibilities of that position. He should have been viewed in the same light as a corrupt corporate executive or a crooked judge. Like the marketplace or the courtroom, the university has its share of scamps.

I do not intend to suggest that most professors are incompetent or immoral. To emphasize the point I offer another sketch, this of a man in his thirties. In less than a decade of activity, he has compiled an extraordinary record of publications and is well on his way to establishing an international reputation. Not only does he attend all his classes, but he also provides extra sessions for those students who may be having difficulty with the course work. He prepares so assiduously for each lecture that his class presentations are virtually publishable. He develops examinations with care and grades them scrupulously. He is available to his students almost every day and encourages them to bring their examinations and term papers for discussion. He also reads papers given him by any departmental colleague and returns them with detailed notes. He attends all faculty meetings and speaks eloquently. He has served on his school's curriculum committee, played a major role in rethinking collegewide requirements, and almost single-handedly revised his school's manner of handling cases of academic dishonesty. He plays an equally active role in all departmental matters.

Let me emphasize that this man's commitment to his calling is not unique: among his departmental colleagues alone are several others equally devoted to their students, subject, and school.

During my undergraduate years at Columbia College, the faculty included such eminent scholars and dedicated teachers as Jacques Barzun, Daniel Bell, Donald Frame, Charles Frankel, Peter Gay, Moses Hadas, Gilbert Highet, Richard Hofstadter, Polykarp Kusch, Ernest Nagel, Meyer Schapiro, and Lionel Trilling. Surely this esteemed group could have been considered, in Professor X's words, "the guardian of wisdom and Western civilization."

Professors may be dull or lazy, foolish or unethical. They may also be brilliant and indefatigable, wise and even saintly. Some are stereotypically absentminded, but others are extraordinarily perceptive. Some were not suited for success elsewhere and retreated to the groves of academia. Others, however, could have had outstanding careers in medicine, law, or business but chose instead the life of a professor.

Such a choice would not have been made on financial grounds. But it might well have been based on finding joy in teaching and learning, as well as on relishing the independence so characteristic of faculty members. After all, few institutions other than colleges and universities permit their members the latitude so much a part of the professor's life.

Tenured professors normally set their own schedules. They teach virtually when they want, what they want, and how they want. They keep whichever office hours they want, attend such faculty meetings as they want, and accept committee assignments to the extent they want.

To appreciate how ingrained such privileges can become, consider a senior professor of my acquaintance who had managed to reduce his schedule to the minimum, appearing in school only on Friday afternoons to teach two graduate seminars separated by one office hour. Scheduling the classes on Friday afternoons, he had hoped, would minimize the number of students who would enroll. One spring day he was called to his department head's office and asked whether, as a service to students, he might be willing to teach one of his seminars the following fall on Monday afternoons. The suggestion horrified him, and he replied incredulously, "If you don't have Mondays off, what do you have?"

Few attorneys, engineers, or business managers can think in such terms. Indeed, most people, whether they work at honored professions or at low-prestige occupations, are typically required to be at the workplace from morning until night, assuming tasks they have not specifically chosen, under the scrutiny of others who assess their performance and to whom they are responsible. This pattern applies equally to vice presidents at General Motors, to their executive secretaries, and to workers on their assembly lines.

I am not forgetting those professors who work almost every waking hour, seven days a week, ever increasing their depth of understanding and continually adding to their scholarly accomplishments. The crucial point is that these individuals freely decide their schedules and their goals; they do not do so in response to organizational demands. Such an extraordinary degree of faculty autonomy leads into an ethical thicket.

How much faculty autonomy is warranted? And how can we ensure professional conduct without undermining appropriate autonomy?

As a step toward answering the first of these questions, we need to remember that the essence of the professor's life is the pursuit of knowledge. This search may take unexpected turns and lead to dark corners where lie unpopular, controversial, even heretical opinions. But as John Stuart Mill wrote,

> The only way in which a human being can make some approach to knowing the whole of a subject is by hearing what can be said about it by persons of every variety of opinion, and studying all modes in which it can be looked at by every character of mind. No wise man ever acquired his wisdom in any mode but this; nor is it in the nature of human intellect to become wise in any other manner.[2]

The success of a democratic community depends in great part on the understanding and capability of its citizens; thus members of a free society need to ensure that those appointed to seek knowledge and communicate it to others are not interfered with on political, religious, or any other grounds. This protection for faculty members has come to be known as "academic freedom," the right of professionally qualified persons to discover, teach, and publish the truth as they see it within their fields of competence.

Where academic freedom is secure, students enter classrooms with the assurance that instructors are espousing their own beliefs, not mouthing some orthodoxy they have been programmed to repeat. Likewise, where academic freedom is secure, no ideological test is imposed to determine who will be appointed to the faculty. Competence, not creed, is the criterion.

Academic freedom is at stake each time an individual or group seeks to exercise intellectual control over a faculty and inhibit its search for truth. The primary obligation of every faculty member is to resist such threats and yield no ground to those who attempt intimidation or domination. A university without academic freedom is unworthy of the name.

Sad to say, faculty members themselves have sometimes endangered academic freedom. One such threat has come from those who have sought to have a school adopt an official stance on issues unrelated to its educational mission. Free inquiry, however, is impeded when certain opinions are officially declared false and others true. Schools are not established to inform the public where a majority of the faculty happen to stand on any issue, be it mathematical, scientific, or political. Whether the ontological argument for the existence of God is sound, or our government's foreign policy mistaken, are matters for discussion, not decree.

The maintenance of free inquiry requires that all points of view be entitled to a hearing. Unfortunately, some faculty members have on occasion disregarded this fundamental principle and attempted to interfere with a presentation by some campus speaker on the grounds they find the speaker's views unpalatable. But so long as an individual remains civil, no one at the university, whether professors, students, or invited guests, should ever be prevented from stating beliefs. No matter how noxious some opinions may be, the greater danger lies in stifling them. When one person's opinion is silenced, no one else's may be uttered in safety.

Some might suppose that those seeking the truth should be shielded from error. The opposite is the case. We fully understand our own views only after they have been subjected to challenge. In Mill's memorable words, "He who knows only his own side of the case, knows little of that."[3]

During the height of the controversy over the United States' involvement in Vietnam, some faculty members and students became so enraged that they shut down campus buildings, disrupted classes, and in other ways forcibly interfered with activities at their schools. Such actions are inimical to the life of the mind. Free inquiry involves the clash of ideas, but a clash of ideas cannot exist amid a clash of forces. Nor is criminal behavior permissible just because it happens to occur on a college campus.

There have always been individuals both outside and inside the university who would stifle free inquiry in the name of some cause that supposedly demands everyone's unthinking allegiance. The principle of academic freedom is intended as a safeguard against such potential interference.

The professorial life is distinguished not only by the latitude it affords and the academic freedom it guarantees, but also by the opportunity it provides to pursue any area of study, regardless of popularity. Nonspecialists, if exposed to a professor's work, might find it boring or pointless, but that judgment need not concern the professor. Widespread acclaim is not the criterion of academic success, and finding one's book on the best-seller list does not amount to an academic triumph. Faculty members may choose to spend their energy conversing with specialists, reading the works of specialists, writing works to be read by specialists, and teaching those who aspire to become specialists. Such single-minded intensity avoids the pitfalls inherent in pandering to public taste and can produce remarkable intellectual accomplishments. An associated danger, however, is that single-mindedness may turn into narrow-mindedness, and intensity into insularity.

Consider the case of one professor who has devoted his life to exegetical study of the writings of the German philosopher Edmund Husserl, the central figure in the movement known as "phenomenology." As a graduate student this professor took many courses on Husserl and eventually wrote his doctoral dissertation on Husserl, has attended conferences each summer on Husserl, and every semester teaches one or even two courses on Husserl. Once when only two students registered for his Husserl seminar, his departmental colleagues asked him to offer instead an introductory course to provide beginning students with an understanding of the nature of philosophical inquiry. He refused indignantly and insisted that the department should teach only small courses on specialized topics such as Husserl and not be bothered with any students other than its own majors. No one, I hasten to add, had the least success in convincing him of the impracticability and irresponsibility of his proposal for reforming the college curriculum.

Professors of his ilk serve as a reminder of why the university is often referred to as an "ivory tower," a haven for those unwilling or unable to cope with practical concerns. This description is a caricature, but even those faculty members who act in accord with it cannot escape their moral obligations.

In short, although the professorial life is remarkably autonomous, it nevertheless entails a wide range of professional responsibilities. These are faced in a variety of settings—in classrooms, departmental meetings, and faculty meetings—and whenever one's advice is sought, one's recommendations are requested, and one's evaluations are needed.

To enumerate these obligations is not to guarantee their fulfillment. But the first step toward discharging duties is to know what they are.

CHAPTER TWO

~

Teaching

The Art of Instruction

Instructors are obligated to guide the learning process. They should be expected to know which material is to be studied and in what order it is best presented. They should also be expected to know how individuals can proceed most productively. In addition, they should be expected to know what constitutes progress and the extent to which each student has achieved it. Students themselves do not have the knowledge; that is why they are students.

Imagine yourself taking a beginning bridge lesson and hearing your instructor inquire whether you would prefer to study finesses or the Vienna Coup. Such a question would be senseless, for a reasonable answer depends on some knowledge of bridge, and if you already had that, you wouldn't be a beginner.

It would be equally inane for your instructor to decide your skill at bidding by asking you to evaluate yourself. Sensible judgments of this sort depend on an expert's insight, and your instructor, not you, is supposed to be the expert. If your instructor doesn't know how good your bidding is, that person should not be your instructor.

A common method of avoiding the responsibilities of a teacher is to pass the buck to students. A former colleague once told me that her

9

class in the history of modern philosophy was going to jump from Leibniz to Kant, leaving out the empiricists Locke, Berkeley, and Hume. When I inquired why she was proceeding so oddly, she replied that she had asked her students to vote, and they had preferred not to read the empiricists.

The truth was that this instructor, knowing little about the empiricists, wanted to omit them but didn't want to be held accountable for such an obvious gap in her course. She tried therefore to absolve herself of responsibility by describing the empiricists in negative terms, then asking her students their preference. She could have persuaded them of virtually anything, for as far as they knew Locke, Berkeley, and Hume might have been the outfield for the 1914 Boston Braves.

A teacher is properly held responsible for what occurs in the classroom, and with responsibility goes authority. Recall that we speak not only of authority as power, but also of *an* authority—that is, an expert. These two concepts are related, for the responsibilities that entail the exercise of authority or power are often assigned to individuals by virtue of presumed authority or expertise.

Such is the case with teachers, for their superior knowledge justifies their being assigned pedagogic responsibilities. To put the matter crassly, if teachers understand a subject no better than their students, why should students be charged tuition while teachers receive paychecks? I have often heard teachers minimize their own importance and emphasize how much they have learned from the insight and imagination of their students, but I have yet to hear a single professor offer to exchange an instructor's salary for a student's bill.

To recognize a teacher's authority, however, is not to suggest that the teacher should act in an authoritarian manner, exercising complete control over the will of students. The appropriate relationship is that of guide, not god.

A useful parallel can be drawn to the proper relationship of a doctor with a patient. A good doctor pays close attention to a patient's reactions and adapts treatment to each individual case. But if urged to prescribe inappropriate medicine, the doctor refuses to do so, recognizing responsibility for the prescription signed. If called on to certify a patient's health, the doctor does so on the basis of generally recognized standards, not on the basis of the patient's own criteria.

The situation is similar to that of a good teacher who pays close attention to a student's reaction and adapts instruction to the individual case. But if urged to discuss material in an inappropriate way, the teacher refuses to do so, recognizing responsibility for the course offered. If called on to certify a student's competence, the teacher does so on the basis of generally recognized standards, not on the basis of the student's own criteria.

Once we recognize the extent to which students are necessarily dependent on their instructors, we realize how much harm faculty members can inflict. Which of us has not felt the sting of a teacher's thoughtless or malicious gibe? Or been victimized by a teacher's carelessness or meanness? Or developed a blindness or aversion to some potentially fascinating subject as a result of a teacher's incompetent, boring, or aberrant presentation?

Teaching thus has an ethical dimension, for the teacher has the capacity to help or harm others. But can we delineate the essentials of good teaching? In recent years, reputedly insightful educators have expressed doubts as to whether anyone knows the characteristics that epitomize a good teacher. At the same time, these same individuals issue an impassioned appeal for the improvement of teaching. Yet they fail to note the contradiction inherent in their position. If we are to encourage good teaching, we need to understand its essentials. And these are by no means impossible to explain.

Put simply, a teacher's responsibility is to lead students to master appropriate subject matter, arousing appreciation for it while neither misrepresenting nor diluting it. To achieve this result typically involves four elements: motivation, organization, clarification, and generalization.

Concerning motivation, I distinguish two types of teachers: those I refer to as pulling the subject matter behind them and those I refer to as pushing the subject matter in front of them. The former use their own personalities to attract students, then try to transfer the students' interest from the instructor to the subject. The latter minimize their own personalities and seek to interest students directly in the material itself.

Those who pull the subject behind them usually have little difficulty in arousing enthusiasm, but their characteristic pitfall is the failure to redirect the students' interest away from the instructor and towards the subject. If, however, they succeed in involving students as much in the material as in the instructor's own manner, they can exert an enormously beneficial influence on an extraordinary number of students, for such teachers invariably attract many devoted admirers who will follow wherever they are led, even down the rugged road of learning.

Those teachers who push the subject in front of them need not worry about misdirecting a student's interest; their worry is whether such interest will be aroused at all. They need to make apparent the connections between seemingly esoteric material and the students' own sphere of experience, so that the subject itself becomes the students' personal concern.

Whatever the particular approach of their instructors, students should be encouraged to appreciate the subject not merely as a means but as an end, something of intrinsic worth to be enjoyed on its own account. Their lives will thereby be enriched, and the material rendered more vivid and even more useful when serving a purpose beyond itself.

A motivated student is ready to learn, but a teacher should be organized enough to take advantage of this situation. Granted, inflexibility can hinder an instructor from making the most of opportunities that may arise spontaneously in the course of discussion. A rambling presentation, however, may well dissipate initial enthusiasm. A lack of planning usually leads to stream-of-consciousness instruction and results in a class that meanders idly from one topic to another, amounting to nothing more than an hour of aimless talk.

Before setting foot inside the classroom, teachers ought to decide exactly what they intend to accomplish during a particular session and precisely what they expect their students to know by the time the period ends. In Alfred North Whitehead's words, "A certain ruthless definiteness is essential in education."[1] A teacher's obligation is to guide students, and to guide requires a sense of where one is headed. If the teacher does not know, everyone is lost.

Careful organization must be complemented by equal concern for clarification. Otherwise, even the most highly structured course of study may prove incomprehensible to the uninitiated.

Because academic subjects tend toward complexity, classrooms are often rife with confusion. Good teachers foresee this problem and reduce it by making every effort to be as clear as possible. They use concrete cases to exemplify abstract concepts. Good teachers also realize that individuals differ in how they arrive at an understanding of particular ideas, and such teachers take pains to explain fundamental principles in a variety of ways.

Furthermore, good teachers direct their remarks not only at the best student, or at the top ten percent of the class, or even at the majority; instead, good teachers speak so that virtually all their listeners can follow. These teachers realize that when more than one or two students complain that they are lost, many others, whether they themselves realize so, also need help.

We come finally to the fourth element of good instruction: generalization. Because a thorough knowledge of any subject matter depends on a firm grasp of its details, the tendency of many instructors is to emphasize analysis at the expense of synthesis. But mastery of a subject requires awareness of its connections to related areas of inquiry. Details are necessary to understanding, but they are not sufficient. Also required is perspective, which can be achieved only by viewing specific information within a broad framework. A student should not be allowed to become lost in minutiae. Generalizations without details are hollow, but details without generalizations are barren.

Thus far I have been considering the components of good teaching. Great teaching involves yet another element. Great teachers not only motivate their students, organize the class, clarify their material, and provide illuminating generalizations. They also project a vision of excellence.

Excellence has become an educational shibboleth, and its mere mention now delights some people while distressing others. These different reactions, however, may stem not from any fundamental disagreement but from an ambiguity lurking in the concept itself.

In one sense excellence is equivalent to superiority. Given this definition, one achieves excellence by surpassing others, however strong or weak the opposition may be. Thus each valedictorian, ranking first among classmates in scholarship, is by definition an excellent student.

In another sense excellence is equivalent to merit. According to this usage, an individual is excellent if worthy of high commendation, regardless of how many others deserve similar praise. For example, we speak of being in excellent health or possessing an excellent moral character. Note that many of us are in excellent health, not just a few. Numerous persons are of excellent moral character, for one individual's noble action does not preclude another's but may encourage it.

Excellence as merit implies a competition against standards; many can win, many can lose. Excellence as superiority implies a competition against others; few can win, most must lose.

Superiority, however, is not necessarily praiseworthy. Consider students who have just been graduated from a very poor medical school. Even the best may not be an effective physician. Superiority is a laudable goal only if accompanied by merit, for to surpass others is a dubious achievement when none is of high quality. Thus the ideal of excellence should be understood as referring to merit, not superiority.

Those who denigrate excellence usually equate it with superiority, and their opposition is based on an antipathy to the ruthlessness too often part of competition. But if in opposing the excesses of bitter rivalry we fail to recognize the difference between what is of high quality and what is not, the result is confusion.

Beginning students, because of unfamiliarity with the fields they are studying, are apt to have little sense of the difference between acceptable and unacceptable work. For this reason, a novice chess player can be impressed by the apparent profundity of superficial combinations. But such naïveté soon vanishes, for how much sophistication is needed to differentiate a weak tennis player from a sound one, a poor violinist from an able performer?

What is not so easy to distinguish, however, even after considerable study, is the difference between what is adequate and what is excellent. How many of us, observing two physicians, would know which was merely competent and which superb? How many of us, reading a history of Europe, would realize whether the account was just satisfactory or exceptional? Recognizing such distinctions depends on an awareness of critical subtleties. Each great teacher, in distinctive and inimitable ways, leads students to acquire such insight.

Those who attain excellence know the sense of satisfaction that accompanies such success. But excellence is of value not only to those who possess it. Its significance is equally important to those who learn to prize it, for by developing the acuity and sensitivity needed to comprehend the magnificent achievements of which human effort is capable, one's perceptions are rendered more vivid and one's experience enormously enriched. Indeed, I know of no greater gift a teacher can bestow than to impart to students an abiding appreciation for excellence.

We should never forget the nobility of the teacher's art. But as in all arts, achievement depends on conscientious attention to details. I turn next to some of these.

A Teacher's Concerns

The terms "conscience," "conscious," and "conscientious" are related not only etymologically, but also conceptually. A teacher with a conscience is one who is conscious of pedagogical details and conscientious in ensuring they are handled properly. Such concern for detail is widely recognized as an element of serious scholarship, but should also be regarded as an element of quality teaching. Some may consider a discussion of mechanics to be petty, but if these matters are neglected, students suffer the consequences.

To see this principle in practice, imagine yourself as a faculty member who has been asked to teach a particular course, perhaps for the first time. What are your specific obligations?

First you should find out how the course is described in the college catalogue or other official listing, for that description is, in essence, a promise to students regarding the content of the course. If you wish, you may eventually be able to rewrite the description. Your responsibility now, however, is to teach the course as announced.

You need to consider which books you will ask the students to purchase. Before making that decision, you should familiarize yourself with alternative texts and editions, evaluating each with regard to difficulty, coverage, and cost. Instructors should never adopt a text they have not themselves read; months later they may discover that it omits necessary materials or presents them inadequately. One can never be certain when using a book for the first time that it will prove entirely satisfactory, but at least the instructor should have carefully studied its contents and made a decision only after serious reflection.

Keep in mind, too, that while a teacher may receive a complimentary copy of an adopted text, students pay for their books, and should not be asked to spend extravagantly to fulfill course requirements. Be sure to check current prices, for a book may cost far more today than it did when it was originally published. I recall one professor in his sixties who for decades had required students to purchase a particular book, never realizing that over the years its price had more than quadrupled while a far less expensive edition of the same work had become available.

I have heard some say that professors should not adopt texts they themselves authored or edited, because they would earn royalties on these required purchases. I see no conflict of interest in this practice, as long as the books chosen are, in fact, the most appropriate. Shouldn't Ralph Ellison, when teaching a course in contemporary literature, have had the right to ask his students to read *Invisible Man*? Whichever books are chosen, someone will earn royalties. The only genuine issue is whether the texts selected are pedagogically justifiable.

Eventually the time comes to prepare a syllabus. This document is the student's guide to the course and should be presented at the first class meeting. It should indicate the assigned readings for each week or each meeting of the course, and specify any deadlines for assignments. While a change in the readings may be necessary during the semester, such alterations should be kept to a minimum, lest students become disoriented and their plans for covering the course material are upset. Any announced deadlines should also be firmly maintained. To give those who are late the same consideration as others is blatantly unfair, misleading to students, and self-defeating for instructors.

A professor of my acquaintance once announced a deadline for submission of term papers, then a week later announced that the deadline had been extended for those who were having trouble meeting the original deadline, and then another week later announced that the deadline had been extended again for those who were having trouble meeting the extended deadline. No one paid attention to any of these deadlines, and the professor spent the final days before commencement frantically grading a bushel of term papers, trying desperately to turn in grades in time for the students to graduate with their classmates. This foolishness was repeated year after year. The point is clear: teachers who fail to show respect for their own rules do not deserve, and will not receive, the respect of others.

Many instructors append to the syllabus a bibliography, listing relevant works that students can consult. The value of such a bibliography is in direct proportion to the quality of the annotation provided. A listing of hundreds of items with no commentary is bewildering and virtually useless. A student has time to consult only a few sources. Which are most important? What purposes might others serve? A bibliography that fails to provide this essential information is hardly worth distributing.

Soon you are ready to plan the first day of classes. Note the word "plan." As mentioned previously, no responsible instructor ever enters the classroom without careful planning. Of course, you can be totally unprepared and still survive the class period, perhaps by asking the students to give their reactions to the assigned readings. To teach in this manner, though, is akin to sight-reading a piano recital: in neither case are the results worth hearing.

Is planning necessary for the initial class meeting? Don't you simply distribute the syllabus, then dismiss the class? Many instructors squander the first session in just this way, only to complain at the end of the semester that they have run out of time. Any lost class is a wasted opportunity, and students are entitled to the full complement of scheduled sessions.

On the first day an instructor can set the tone for the entire course, placing the subject matter in perspective, specifying what will be required of the students, and suggesting how they can most effectively approach their work. Students who come to class to learn but find their first session aborted after only a few minutes are apt to be dismayed, and rightly so, for their instructor has already been derelict in duty.

A simple but important principle is that teachers are obligated to begin all classes on time. I know of no more obvious sign of a lack of concern for one's students than coming to class late and thereby wasting the time of those who have arrived promptly. A teacher who comes late encourages students to come late. Soon everyone is late, and the class periods are shortened. If a class is scheduled to last fifty minutes, then students deserve all fifty minutes, no less.

Furthermore, lost minutes should not be made up by extending the class beyond its scheduled end. Prolonging one class may cause lateness at the next, and students should not miss important material just because they have to leave when the class was supposed to end. A con-scientious teacher begins classes when they are scheduled to begin and ends them when they are scheduled to end. This rule may be obvious, but it is not trivial.

Another such rule is that professors are obliged to be present at every session. If for reasons of the most serious moment they are unable to do so, they should, if possible, arrange for qualified substitutes. Reschedul-ing a class should be a last resort, for invariably some students, because of a conflict, will lose their rightful opportunity to attend.

Professors are also obligated to be available to students for con-sultations outside class. Office hours should be posted, and professors should be present as announced. Failing to appear for office hours, an all-too-common practice, is professorial irresponsibility. Considering the relatively small number of hours per week professors are required to be at school, they should make every effort to attend every scheduled appointment.

Another seemingly simple, yet significant, matter is that students are individuals and appreciate being recognized as such by the use of their names. Extremely large classes make observing this principle dif-ficult. Yet I have known conscientious professors with classes of more than two hundred who cared enough to learn the name of each student.

On the other hand, years ago I asked a colleague about the progress of several of his students, and he turned out to be unaware they were in his class, because, he confessed, he did not know the names of any of his students. His ignorance did not seem to bother him, despite the term's being half over and his class enrollment only twelve. Think how faculty members would react if their college president didn't care to learn their names. Students have similar reactions to professorial aloofness.

Consider next that in almost every course students are required to complete specific assignments. An instructor should take whatever time is necessary to explain these in detail, making clear exactly what is expected. After all, if students do not know what they are supposed to be doing, the fault is not theirs.

"Write a paper on some aspect of the course" is an irresponsible, vague direction, suggesting the professor has been either too lazy to bother thinking about suitable topics or too callous to care whether students become lost. Should the paper be essentially a summary of other literature or a critical study of it? Does the paper depend on research in the library? If so, of what kind? How broad a topic is appropriate? How long should the paper be? Without answers to such questions, students are prone to confusion and dismay.

Such chaos would not result if a professor distributed the following sort of instructions:

> In Book X of Plato's *Republic*, he refers to 'an ancient quarrel' between poetry and philosophy. Drawing on the dialogues we have studied, explain the reasons Plato offers for supposing such a quarrel exists. If you agree with Plato's views, explain why and indicate what you believe are the most promising possibilities for resolving the quarrel. If you do not agree, explain your replies to the strongest counterarguments Plato or others might offer. In preparing the paper, do not consult any sources outside the dialogues themselves. The paper should be approximately 2,000 words in length and is due March 6. No late papers will be accepted.

This assignment is demanding but not bewildering, and students who undertake it will be able to spend their time analyzing the ideas of Plato, not guessing the intentions of their instructor.

Assignments should always be returned with detailed comments. For a student to prepare material carefully, then have it given back with only a brief note such as "C: good try" is utterly disheartening. Students are entitled to be informed which aspects of their work are well done and which unsatisfactory, as well as how future efforts might be improved. Faculty members with no interest in providing such guidance have chosen the wrong profession.

Assignments should also be returned to students within a reasonably short time. Otherwise, in preparing further assignments the students will be unable to utilize the instructor's suggestions, and may even stop caring about the whole matter once they have begun to forget the patterns of thinking that structured their work. Sometimes outside a professor's office one sees a box of students' papers, handed in months before and finally corrected by the instructor, but never retrieved by those who wrote them. This sad sight is evidence of professorial negligence and student alienation.

I have yet to mention the two areas of a faculty member's responsibility that demand the most conscientious attention to detail: examinations and grades. Professors remiss in handling these critical matters may not only disconcert students, but also do them harm. In recent years much controversy has surrounded the use of these instruments of evaluation, and so I shall discuss in depth the purposes they serve, the ways they have been misused, and the procedures for employing them effectively.

Examinations

If teachers are to guide the learning process, they need to know whether students are making progress. Examinations are a key tool for making this determination, because their purpose is to assess the scope and depth of a student's knowledge. Just as athletes are tested under game conditions and musicians under concert conditions, so students are tested under examination conditions to reveal whether they are in complete control of certain material or possess only a tenuous grasp of it. To speak glibly about a subject is not nearly as indicative of one's knowledge as to reply without prompting to pertinent questions and commit those answers to paper so they can be scrutinized by experts.

Nor is writing term papers an adequate substitute for taking examinations. Rarely do such papers require mastery of most or even much of the course material. Moreover, help is obtainable outside the classroom from sources unavailable within. For those reasons, almost all students, given the choice, opt for writing a paper rather than taking an examination. For those same reasons responsible instructors do not offer students that inappropriate choice.

The use of examinations has been criticized on the grounds that the implicit pressure prevents students from doing their best work. But pressure is inherent in any situation in which individuals are called on to prove their competence. The golfer who appears impressive at the practice tee but performs poorly during competitive rounds lacks command of the requisite skills. Similarly, the student who sounds knowledgeable in conversation but performs poorly in examinations lacks command of the requisite knowledge.

Another criticism of examinations is that they emphasize the acquisition of factual knowledge instead of encouraging creative thought. But mastery of any significant field of inquiry requires control of basic information and skills. As Alfred North Whitehead observed, "To write poetry you must study metre: and to build bridges you must be learned in the strength of material. Even the Hebrew prophets had learned to write, probably in those days requiring no mean effort. The untutored art of genius is—in the words of the Prayer Book—a vain thing, fondly invented."[2] Examinations are not the best test of imaginative power, but to suppose that original thinking flows from those ignorant of relevant fundamentals is unrealistic. These are the focus of effective examinations.

I turn now to the details of constructing such examinations. First, they should always be representative of the course material. If, for instance, a survey of the nineteenth-century British novel is devoted equally to the works of Jane Austen, Charles Dickens, George Eliot, and Thomas Hardy, the final examination should be structured so that students are required to demonstrate considerable knowledge about all four. The examination would be unsatisfactory if it tested only the students' generalized skills of literary criticism but not their knowledge of the four authors. Nor should the examination allow students to exhibit understanding of only one or two, for such an examination would not then be a fair test of a student's knowledge of the entire subject.

Effective examinations pose questions that require detailed answers. Without this safeguard students can engage in circumlocution and thereby camouflage the limits of their knowledge. Demonstrating mastery of subject matter demands more than offering stray bits of information and undefined concepts strung together by vague generalizations. An examination that can be passed by offering such feeble answers is an educational travesty and worse than no examination at all, for it may mislead students into believing they have learned material about which they know virtually nothing.

To emphasize the importance of requiring detailed answers is not to suggest that students be overwhelmed with multiple-choice questions. Although these can sometimes be of value, unless they are well-constructed and appropriate to the aims of a course, they can turn an examination into a guessing game that stresses knowledge of trivia rather than an understanding of fundamental ideas and principles. For example, only a foolish examination in the history of modern philosophy would be filled with questions such as "The title of Section IX of Hume's *An Enquiry Concerning Human Understanding* is (a) Of Liberty, (b) Of the Reason of Animals, (c) Of Miracles, (d) All of the above, (e) None of the above." But to ask: "Does it seem to you that anything in the work of Kant helps us to understand ourselves?" would be equally foolish.

What is needed is neither a trivial nor formless question but a sharply focused, significant, challenging question such as: "Both Descartes and Berkeley raise doubts about the existence of the material world. Compare and contrast the arguments they use to raise these doubts and their conclusions concerning the possible resolution of these doubts." Answering such a question requires genuine mastery of subject matter, not merely the memorization of trifles or the improvisation of hazy, high-flown vacuities.

A common pitfall in constructing an examination is to make it so long that students are more worried about finishing than about providing the best possible answers. Admittedly, students who take too long to answer a question do not have secure control of the material, but an examination should not be a race against time. Students working at a normal pace should be able to read the questions carefully, think about them, write legible answers, and reread them to make corrections. If time is not available for these steps, the examination serves no useful purpose.

Another pitfall is the omission of clear directions at the top of the examination sheet. Imagine sitting down to begin work and reading the following instructions: "Answer three questions from Part I and two questions from Part II, but do not answer questions 2, 3, and 6 unless you also answer question 9. Question 1 is required, unless you answer questions 3 and 5." By the time students have fully understood these directions and decided which questions to answer, they will already be short of time.

Teachers have the responsibility to make the instructions so clear that misunderstanding is virtually impossible. Students who take an examination are understandably tense and liable to misread the directions, answer the wrong questions, and bungle the proceedings. An examination should test knowledge of subject matter, not the ability to solve verbal puzzles.

An additional pitfall is failing to inform students of the relative importance of each answer in the grading of the examination. Suppose students are required to answer three questions but are not told that the instructor considers answers to the third question more important than the combined answers to the first two. Students may spend an equal amount of time on each, never realizing they should concentrate time and effort on the third. Their mistake would indicate no lack of knowledge about the subject but would result from the faculty member's keeping the scoring system a secret. Fairness dictates that students be informed how much each question is worth, so they can plan their work accordingly.

For an examination to fulfill its proper purposes, it must be graded as carefully and fairly as possible. Doing otherwise wastes the effort put into its construction.

One helpful technique is to grade each test without knowing its author. An answer from a regularly good student may seem more impressive than the same answer from a regularly poor one. Also advisable is not to grade tests by reading them from start to finish, but by reading all students' answers to one question at a time. A teacher will thus be sure to pay close attention to each answer a student gives rather than skimming a test after perusing only one or two responses. Furthermore, correcting tests this way lessens the possibility that a teacher will alter standards from one test to another, because stabilizing standards for answers to the same question is far easier than doing so for entire tests. Before grading any questions, teachers should list for themselves the major points they expect students to include in their answers, so that each essay can be checked against this list, thereby providing another safeguard against altering standards from one test to the next.

As with term papers, examinations should be graded with comments and returned promptly. Students eagerly await the outcome and, especially if they have not done well, need to become aware of their problems as soon as possible. Faculty members who procrastinate, whether from laziness or indifference, and return examinations after many weeks or even months are guilty of misconduct.

For obvious reasons, most faculty members prefer reading and writing books rather than developing examinations. Far more fascinating activities can be found than reviewing numerous answers to the same question and deciding how many points each is worth. Yet teachers owe their students the time and effort to frame each examination with care and grade it conscientiously. Whether teachers do so is a clear indication of how committed they are to the ideals of their profession.

Grades

Of all a teacher's duties, none has aroused as much controversy as the practice of grading students. Grades have been said to be inherently inaccurate devices that, in attempting to measure people, only traumatize and dehumanize them. This charge is a tangle of misconceptions.

A grade is intended to represent an expert's judgment of the quality of a student's work within a specified area of inquiry. Such information can be useful in a variety of ways: as a basis for determining whether a student should be permitted to continue in school, be granted a degree, or be awarded academic honors; as a guide for advising students or deciding on their admission to other institutions; and as an aid to students themselves in judging their past efforts, assessing their present abilities, or formulating their future plans.

Would these functions be better fulfilled if, as some have suggested, grades were replaced by letters of evaluation? In addition to the impracticality of a professor's writing hundreds of individual comments and the members of a committee reading thousands, such letters would be of limited value unless they included specific indications of students' levels of performance, in other words, the equivalent of grades. Otherwise, the letters would be more likely to reveal the teachers' literary styles than the students' academic accomplishments. Remarks one instructor considers high praise may be used indiscriminately by another, while comments intended as mild commendation may be taken as tempered criticism. The advantage of grades is that they are limited in number and standardized in meaning. Professors who employ them idiosyncratically are not victims of linguistic ambiguity but perpetrators of pedagogic fraud.

While a piece of work would not necessarily be graded identically by all specialists, members of the same discipline usually agree whether a student's performance has been outstanding, good, fair, poor, or unsatisfactory, the levels of achievement commonly symbolized by "A, B, C, D, F." Of course, experts in any field may sometimes clash, but in doing so they do not obliterate the crucial distinction between their knowledgeable judgments and a novice's uninformed impressions.

What of the oft-repeated charge that grades are impersonal devices that reduce people to letters of the alphabet? This criticism is misguided. A grade is not a measure of a person but of a person's level of achievement in a particular course of study. Students who receive C's in introductory physics are not C persons with C personalities or C moral characters, but individuals who have achieved only a fair grasp of the fundamentals of elementary physics.

Grades no more reduce students to letters than batting averages reduce baseball players to numbers. That Ted Williams had a lifetime batting average of .344 and Joe Garagiola one of .257 does not mean Williams was a better person than Garagiola, only that Williams was a better hitter. Surely respect for our fellow human beings does not require resorting to the obvious fiction that everyone is excellent at everything.

Do grades foster competition? Obviously, many people have goals that only comparatively few can attain; not everyone can succeed as a surgeon, a movie star, or a professional basketball player. Thus, competition arises. And, surprising as it may seem, its effects are often beneficial. As Gilbert Highet observed,

> It is sad, sometimes, to see a potentially brilliant pupil slouching through his work, sulky and willful, wasting his time and thoughts on trifles, because he has no real equals in his own class; and it is heartening to see how quickly, when a rival is transferred from another section or enters from another school, the first boy will find a fierce joy in learning and a real purpose in life.[3]

Any scheme for eliminating all competition is unrealistic. But grades, if awarded fairly, will contribute to fair competition, a worthy ideal.

Much discussion has taken place about alternative grading systems, but the basic principle for constructing an effective system remains simple: it should contain the maximum number of levels teachers can use consistently. Up to that point, the more detailed the system, the more helpful the information it provides. My experience has led me to conclude that in college the most effective grading system is the traditional one, consisting of ten symbols: A, A−, B+, B, B−, C+, C, C−, D, F. This system is specific enough to provide needed information about a student's level of achievement while enabling instructors to differentiate consistently between work on any two levels. Borderline cases will arise; nonetheless, the distinction between levels remains clear.

The single most disputed aspect of the traditional grading system is the mark of F. To preclude a student's receiving such a disheartening evaluation, some college faculties have replaced that grade with NC (No Credit), which indicates to the registrar both that the student should receive no credit for the course and that the transcript should show no record of the student's having taken the course. But that grade is deceptive, for the student did take the course and failed to master any significant part of it. A person who requires two, three, or four attempts to pass calculus lacks the mathematical or study skills of someone who passes the first time, and such a problem should not be hidden from those examining a student's record. Failures are not fatal, but we should learn from them, not rename them and pretend they never occurred. As a former colleague of mine remarked during a faculty meeting at which the NC grade was being debated: "When I die and stand before the heavenly judge in order to have my life evaluated, it may be that I shall receive a grade of F. But let it not be said that my life was a 'No Credit.'"

A fair grading system, however, does not ensure fair grading. That depends on a professor's conscientiousness about applying the system properly. One potential misuse is to award grades on bases other than a student's level of achievement. Irrelevant criteria include a student's sex, race, religion, nationality, physical appearance, dress, personality, attitudes, innate capacities, and previous academic record. None of these factors should even be considered in deciding a student's grade. Performance in the course should be the only test.[4]

The most effective means for assuring students that no extraneous factors will enter into grading is for the instructor to make clear at the beginning of the term how final grades will be determined. How much will the final examination count? How about the term paper and other short assignments and quizzes? What of laboratory work? Will a student's participation in class discussion be a factor? Answering these questions at the outset enables students to concentrate their energies on the most important aspects of the course, not waste time speculating about the professor's intentions.

Another misuse of the grading system is the practice commonly referred to as "grading on a curve." The essence of this scheme is for the instructor to decide before the course begins what percentage of students will receive each grade. This method may produce aesthetically pleasing designs on a graph, but is nevertheless conceptually confused. While a student's achievement should be judged in the light of reasonable expectations, these do not depend on such haphazard circumstances as the mix of students who happen to be taking the course simultaneously.

Consider the plight of a student who earns an eighty on an examination but receives a D, because most classmates scored higher. Yet the following year in the same course another student earns an eighty on the same examination and receives an A, because this time almost all classmates scored lower. Two students, identical work, different grades: the system is patently unfair.

Why, then, do so many instructors resort to this approach? Because by doing so they avoid the responsibility of determining the quality of the work each grade represents. They also are free to construct examinations without worrying about skewed results, because even if the highest grade is thirty-five out of one hundred, grading on a curve will yield apparently acceptable consequences. Yet the appearance is deceiving, because rank in class will have been confused with mastery of subject matter. The Procrustean practice of grading on a curve rests on this muddle and therefore ought to be abandoned.

A different distortion of the grading system, rare nowadays, is an unwillingness to award high grades. Instructors who adopt this attitude take pride in rigor. But just as a third grade student who receives an A in writing need not be the literary equal of a college freshman who receives an A in composition, so a freshman may deserve an A without being the literary equal of Jonathan Swift or George Orwell. The award of an A does not signify that a student has learned everything knowable about the course material, only that, considering what can reasonably be expected, the student has done excellent work. An instructor who rarely awards high grades is failing to distinguish good from poor work. Such irresponsibility does not uphold academic standards but only misinterprets the grading symbols, thus undermining their appropriate functions.

I turn next to the misuse of the grading system that became so prevalent during the 1960s and remains today the most serious threat to its usefulness: the reluctance to award low grades, a practice popularly known as "grade inflation." Decades ago, when the phrase "gentleman's C" was in vogue, C was entirely respectable, reflecting an adequate performance. B was commendable, indicating good work. A was a symbol of excellence, signifying outstanding achievement. Today those meanings have changed. C suggests poor performance, B corresponds to the once-traditional C, and A is awarded to work that in the past would have received either A or B. Thus the present grading system lacks a clear mark of excellence, and students may thereby be deprived of an appreciation of that ideal.

What caused grade inflation? The answer lies in the temper of those times, perhaps most clearly encapsulated in Charles A. Reich's 1970 best-seller, *The Greening of America*. He described the younger generation as "reject[ing] the whole concept of excellence and comparative merit," and offered the following defense of that viewpoint: "Each person has his own individuality, not to be compared to that of anyone else. Someone may be a brilliant thinker, but he is not 'better' at thinking than anyone else, he simply possesses his own excellence. A person who thinks very poorly is still excellent in his own way."[5]

If all agree that one individual is a brilliant thinker and another thinks poorly, then to maintain that the first is no better at thinking than the second is contradictory. Despite Reich's optimism, the second may not possess any notable virtues. In that case he would not be "excellent in his own way"; he would not be excellent in any way.

To dwell on such obvious points misses the extraordinary mood of those years. Campuses were besieged by bands of rioting students. While the major incentive for the call to activism was the Vietnam War, longstanding issues such as minority rights and student freedoms were also prominent. The quintessential opponent was "the power structure," in all its governmental, industrial, and social manifestations. Authority was to be torn down, power to be returned to "the people." Universities were viewed as in alliance with that power structure, indoctrinating those who would eventually control society. Protestors connected the nation they perceived as engaging in social and political oppression with the educational institutions they saw as fostering bitter competition among students imprisoned within archaic academic traditions. Therefore, colleges, at first only the site of attacks against governmental policies, became themselves the target of attacks by groups who considered forays against the educational establishment to be direct blows against "the system."

Throughout the 1960s protestors called for an end to all discrimination. At first these demands were directed against discrimination on the basis of race, sex, or nationality. But when the response of universities appeared insufficient, the academic power structure came to be considered not only a political enemy but also a moral enemy. So another form of discrimination came under attack: discrimination on the basis of achievement.

This misguided version of egalitarianism, mirrored by Reich, refused to accept judgments of merit. Grades were considered oppressive; degrees and awards were said to be trappings of elitism, the worst of sins. Under this pressure, college faculties around the country lowered expectations, abolished examinations, and either discarded grades altogether or nullified them through rampant inflation.

Some professors stood their ground and fought to maintain academic standards, but many, whether from confusion or cowardice, ignored their responsibilities and abandoned any concern for quality. As a result American higher education lost its sense of purpose and suffered what I then termed "the eclipse of excellence."[6]

Recovery began some years later, but grade inflation persists, in part because instructors are concerned about the possible injustice of giving their own students realistic grades while other students receive inflated grades. Yet the solution to this problem is simple and has been adopted at a number of colleges, where transcripts now include not only a student's course grade but also the average grade of all students in the course. In this way grade inflation is publicly exposed, and an unfair advantage from it is dissipated.

The time is long overdue for professors to return to the proper use of the grading system, and to award students the grades they deserve. In so doing faculty members will be fulfilling one of their most important responsibilities: to provide accurate evaluations.

A Teacher's Role

Having emphasized the importance of attending to pedagogical details, I now turn to the broader issue of the proper relationship between teacher and student, and the pitfalls instructors face.

One danger is to allow their pedagogical authority to tempt them into talking and acting as if their judgments were beyond reproach. Remember that faculty members typically hold sway in their classrooms without the threat of serious intellectual challenge. The professor lectures to the class and the students busily take notes, seeking to comprehend complexities mastered long before by the professor, and hoping to gain favor and a high grade. Students tend to ask elementary questions, and the instructor replies as easily as a table tennis champion returning a beginner's serve. Under these circumstances, faculty members can easily become enamored of their own erudition.

Another factor that encourages such an attitude is that, unlike most other professionals, college teachers deal mainly with young people, who have limited experience and accomplishments. Professors are apt to have a far wider and deeper background than any of their students, and so they are especially susceptible to delusions of grandeur. But like everyone else, professors are ignorant about many fields of endeavor, and even within their own areas of specialty are subject to error. They should never lead students to suppose otherwise.

Indeed, whenever a faculty member states opinions not shared by other reputable scholars, students ought to be so informed. They are entitled to know whether their teacher is expressing a consensus or only a majority or minority viewpoint. For an instructor to defend personal beliefs is appropriate, but serious alternatives should not be neglected. A faculty member should consider this question: if another qualified instructor were in my place, might that individual offer opinions that conflict with those I have presented? If the answer is yes, the faculty member should alert students, thereby increasing their understanding of the relevant issue.

For example, when teaching introductory philosophy I discuss the traditional problem of free will and determinism. The issue, in brief, is whether determinism, the thesis that every state of affairs is caused by a preceding one, is logically compatible with free will, the thesis that at least some of a person's actions are performed without constraint. If our choices to perform actions are caused by other factors, which are themselves caused by others, and so on, then are the actions free?

My own view is that determinism and free will are incompatible—that one or the other is false, although to say which is not easy. Most contemporary philosophers, however, believe that the two doctrines are compatible, an opinion shared by many noted philosophers of the past, including Hobbes, Hume, and Mill. In presenting the problem to students, therefore, I argue for my own view but emphasize that it is a minority opinion. I also do my best to explain as persuasively as possible the arguments that have been offered by those who disagree with me.

Just as opposing positions should not be disregarded, so they should not be distorted. An instructor is well-advised to imagine that intellectual opponents are in the classroom while the instructor presents their viewpoints. Would the opponents recognize the instructor's version? And would they agree that at least some of their arguments had been adequately explained? If not, the instructor should be making greater efforts to be fair to the opposition.

Professors who are partisans usually display this failure in their manner of responding to questions. Instead of encouraging each student to think independently and raise challenges, they engage in intimidation and expect acquiescence. Their aim is not education but indoctrination. Such attempts to foster ideological zeal may be in order at a political rally but are entirely inappropriate in a college classroom. Teachers should be guiding a critical inquiry, and an essential feature of this process is for all participants, including the faculty member, to be open-minded.

Open-mindedness, however, should not be confused with empty-headedness. Responsible instructors do not sit by passively and permit students to trash academic standards. The wrong approach is that suggested by O. B. Hardison in his 1972 book, *Toward Freedom and Dignity*, a work reflecting views prevalent at that time. He refers to his professorial role as that of "the net in an intellectual tennis game."[7] He tells of the occasion when he arranged for his class to be taught by a two-person team of students, then found their presentation "wretched" and filled with "blatant hypocrisy and grotesque parody." What did he do? "I puffed my pipe. At the end of the session, I arose, clapped students A and B on the back, and expressed gratification over their fine performance."[8] Something is seriously amiss with an educational theory that in the name of human dignity countenances such instances of unabashed deceit.

Students should not be led to suppose that all expressed opinions are equally sound. Some arguments are valid, some invalid. Some hypotheses are well-founded, some not. A claim may be self-contradictory, it may run counter to the available evidence, its meaning may be unclear, or it may mean nothing at all. Educated persons do not simply hold beliefs; they believe what they can explain and cogently defend.

Not every piece of work is good. In fact, some work is no good at all. Individuals may be amiable, cooperative, and sensitive to the needs of humanity, but they may nevertheless produce jumbled economics papers or incompetent laboratory reports. Good intention is no justification for inadequate performance. Admirable goals do not obliterate the differences between clarity and obscurity, accuracy and carelessness, knowledge and ignorance. Responsible instructors insist on these distinctions.

Overlooking them may sometimes result from misunderstanding the professor's role. Hardison, for example, supposes that a class has "obvious affinities to a sensitivity group" and that good teaching has a "kinship to therapy."[9] For a person whose advanced degree is in English, economics, or engineering to attempt to act as a clinical psychologist is both foolish and dangerous. A student undergoing an emotional crisis should be sent to the school's counseling service, not treated by a medical tyro, however well-meaning. College professors do not presume to practice surgery; they should also refrain from psychiatry.

One other misconception about the proper relationship between teacher and student demands special attention, having been the source of some of the most egregious instances of professorial malfeasance. I refer to the view that teachers ought to be friends with their students. What is wrong with this approach, Sidney Hook pointed out, is that a teacher

> must be friendly without becoming a friend, although he may pave the way for later friendship, for friendship is a mark of preference and expresses itself in indulgence, favors, and distinctions that unconsciously find an invidious form. . . .
>
> A teacher who becomes "just one of the boys," who builds on personal loyalty in exchange for indulgent treatment, has missed his vocation. He should leave the classroom for professional politics.[10]

Faculty members ought to care about the progress of each student, but they should remain dispassionate, able to deliberate, judge, and act without thought of personal interest or advantage. Even the appearance of partiality is likely to impair the learning process by damaging an instructor's credibility, causing students to doubt that standards are being applied fairly.

Thus every teacher should be scrupulous in ensuring that no student receives preferential treatment. If one student is permitted to write a paper instead of taking an examination, that option should be available to everyone in the class. If one student is allowed to turn in an assignment late, then all others in similar circumstances should be offered the same opportunity. And if one student in a seminar is invited to the professor's home for dinner, then all others should receive invitations.

One obvious implication of this principle of equal consideration is that between teacher and student not only is friendship inappropriate but, *a fortiori*, so is romance. Even if a student is not enrolled in a professor's class and never intends to be, their liaison suggests to other members of the academic community that this faculty member does not view students from a professional standpoint. If an attempt is made to keep the liaison secret, the professor's integrity is compromised. In any case, such efforts at concealment almost always fail, thus besmirching the professor's reputation for honesty.

If a student seeks to initiate an affair with a professor, the only proper response is an unequivocal refusal. On the other hand, for a professor to attempt to seduce or coerce a student into having an affair is an egregious abuse of authority that provides strong grounds for dismissal.

Indeed, faculty members who tolerate such irresponsible behavior by colleagues are themselves guilty of irresponsibility.

When a student is graduated from school or no longer enrolled in that unit of the university, whatever personal contact may develop with a professor is up to the two of them. But during the years of undergraduate or graduate study, the only appropriate relationship between teacher and student is professional. To maintain these bounds is in everyone's best interest.

In sum, a faculty member ought to guide students through a field of study, not seek to be their psychiatrist, friend, or lover. And guidance should never be corrupted by dogmatism or vitiated by permissiveness.

Evaluating Teaching

Because the proper role of faculty members is to guide the learning process, their authority to do so must be respected and protected. This authority may be threatened in various ways, the most flagrant of which is the attempt to dictate the opinions they espouse. A more subtle, yet equally serious, threat is posed by the widespread practice of judging an instructor's pedagogic skill primarily on the basis of evaluations prepared by students.

The early 1960s saw the first appearance on campuses of faculty-evaluation booklets put together by a few enterprising undergraduates. Originally an amusing novelty, these light-hearted compilations were intended to help those registering for courses by providing tips about the more and less interesting members of the faculty. By the early 1970s these informal reactions had been transformed into complex statistics, obtained by formal procedures and relied on heavily by administrators to help decide an instructor's reappointment, promotion, and even tenure. The rationale for instituting such a system was that when faculty members fail to fulfill their obligations, students suffer the consequences. Shouldn't students, therefore, have a strong voice in evaluating faculty members?

This line of reasoning is fallacious. When airplane pilots fail to fulfill their obligations, passengers often suffer the consequences, but passengers should not have a strong voice in evaluating pilots. A plane has a rough landing. Was the pilot at fault? Simply being a passenger does not enable one to know.

Some proponents of student ratings have argued that learners are the best evaluators of their own responses, drawing an analogy to the restaurant patron who is a better judge of the food than the chef. But while those who eat surely know how the food tastes, its nutritional benefit is judged most reliably by a nutritionist, just as educational value is best judged by an educator.

Students, by definition, do not know the subject matter they are studying, so they are in a poor position to judge how well it is being taught. Perhaps they find a concept difficult to grasp. Is the instructor to blame, or is the difficulty intrinsic to the material? Can the matter be explained more effectively? Perhaps not. An apparently easier way may be only a distortion.

During my first year of high school, the algebra teacher was a gentleman of pompous manner who by his own admission had little knowledge of mathematics beyond the high school level. His presentations were aimed primarily at the weakest students in the class. As one with some bent for the subject, I found the sessions plodding and regularly complained that we were not learning enough.

In my last year I studied trigonometry, and my lively instructor had an apparently firm grasp of the higher reaches of the subject. His presentations were aimed primarily at the strongest students in the class, and the sessions moved rapidly. I was delighted.

Today I can barely remember the basics of trigonometry, but I can solve all sorts of algebra problems with ease. What seemed at the time a useless repetition of basics actually provided a firm grasp of essential skills, while what appeared initially exciting proved in the long run to be cursory and of little lasting value. I had been learning while assuming I was not, and not learning while assuming I was.

Such mistakes can happen easily. How is a student, not knowing the material, to realize whether the instructor's presentation is shallow, inaccurate, incomplete, or biased? Granted, students are a convenient source for easily verifiable matters such as whether teachers hold class regularly, return examinations without delay, provide detailed comments on term papers, and make themselves available for consultation outside the classroom. Students are not in a position to judge whether a teacher is presenting material competently, or to predict, as I could not, whether methods of instruction will prove valuable years after graduation. Students know if teachers are likable, not if they are knowledgeable; they know if lectures are enjoyable, not if they are reliable.

Consider this question that appeared on a widely used evaluation form: "Does the instructor discuss recent developments in the field?" How are students expected to know the sources of the information a teacher offers? Even if something is described to them as a recent development in the field, they are still in the dark as to whether that material is either recent or significant.

Several years ago an experiment was carried out under controlled conditions to test the hypothesis that learners could be seriously mistaken about their teacher's competence.[11] A distinguished-looking professional actor with an authoritative manner was selected to present a lecture to several groups of educators, among them psychiatrists, psychologists, and social workers. They were told they would be hearing a talk by Dr. Myron L. Fox, an expert on the application of mathematics to human behavior. His address was titled "Mathematical Game Theory as Applied to Physician Education." The actor was coached "to present his topic and conduct his question-and-answer period with an excessive use of double talk, neologies, *non sequiturs*, and contradictory statements. All this was to be interspersed with parenthetical and meaningless references to unrelated topics."

At the end of the one-hour lecture and subsequent half-hour discussion, a questionnaire was distributed to the listeners, inquiring what they thought of Dr. Fox. Here are some of their responses: "Excellent presentation, enjoyed listening. Has warm manner. Good flow, seems enthusiastic. Lively examples. Extremely articulate. Good analysis of subject that has been personally studied before. He was certainly captivating. Knowledgeable." My favorite reply was offered by one participant who found the presentation "too intellectual." Most important, all the listeners had many more favorable than unfavorable responses, and not one saw through the hoax. The authors' conclusion was that "students' satisfaction with learning may represent little more than the illusion of having learned."

I once passed a college bulletin board that announced a meeting called by students to demand a greater role in the evaluation of faculty members. The sign declared: "The Administration Must Think We're Stupid." But, as is clear from the Dr. Fox case, what is at issue is not the aptitude of students but their expertise in particular subject matter. Those educators fooled by the actor were surely intelligent, but because they knew little about the material he was supposedly discussing, they were in a weak position to evaluate his performance.

A primary reason schools rely so heavily on student evaluations is the widespread assumption than an impressive body of research data supports the reliability of these ratings. Yet the weight of the evidence suggests that students' judgments may be significantly influenced by considerations other than teaching skills. Here is the conclusion of a survey of the relevant literature:

> Most research on student ratings of teachers does not indicate that the ratings measure the effectiveness of teaching, good teaching, intellectual achievement, nor understanding of basic concepts. The ratings appear to be measuring student satisfaction, the attitudes of students toward their teachers and classes, the psychosocial needs of the student, and the personality characteristics, popularity, and speaking quality of the teacher.[12]

Admittedly, student ratings yield quantifiable results that can easily be given the appearance of exactitude. For example, I have before me a computer-generated spreadsheet, typical of those provided each semester to faculty members at many colleges. It indicates that in a particular course, on a scale of 1 to 5, the instructor scored 4.85 for "Mastery of Subject," while the average for instructors for all sections of the course was 4.67; for all courses in the department the average was 4.60; for all courses in the school it was 4.62. Whatever trust the credulous might place in such pseudo-precise statistics, note that the course in which this instructor received a superior rating for her knowledge was English composition. Sending such inane data to faculty members with the understanding that their scores will play a significant role in the consideration of their reappointment, promotion, or tenure is demeaning to all involved.

A reasonable method of evaluating instructors is observation in the classroom by various faculty members from the same discipline, chosen on the basis of their own outstanding teaching performance. Some instructors may object to such visits from professional colleagues, but I have never heard of any teacher who prohibited the presence of auditors, friends or relatives of students, and even faculty members from other departments. Why, then, should doors be closed to those most qualified to understand what is going on?

Just as physicians may observe one another's procedures, so teachers should be permitted to observe one another's classes. Instituting such a policy would be the simplest, most effective step that could be taken to put instructors on their mettle, afford them the benefit of their colleagues' informed reactions, and dramatically improve the quality of both undergraduate and graduate teaching.

Our suspicions would rightly be aroused by any surgeon who barred all other surgeons from an operation. We should view with equal skepticism any professor who locks classroom doors against any knowledgeable observers.

Evaluating a teacher primarily on the basis of student opinion is not only inappropriate but also dangerous. As Charles Frankel observed, "Teaching is a professional relationship, not a popularity contest. To invite students to participate in the selection or promotion of their teachers . . . exposes the teacher to intimidation."[13] Teachers must never work in fear of their students, for a teacher is expected to question students' pet beliefs, expose their prejudices, challenge them with demanding assignments, and evaluate their work rigorously. Teachers afraid of their students might as well pack briefcases and go home; they cannot educate those they fear. Seeking to propitiate students—granting them favors in exchange for their support—is disgraceful, and no one should be put in a position that encourages such shameful conduct.

Not coincidentally, the increasing use of student evaluations occurred at the same time as grade inflation. If teachers' livelihoods depend on the degree of their popularity with students, self-interest dictates that they award their students high grades. After all, which of us is not inclined to take a more favorable view of those whom we know take a favorable view of us? Are we not likewise apt to be less than enamored of those from whom we receive cool treatment? To be blunt, students who fail a course are hardly likely to award the teacher their highest accolades.

This biasing effect of grades on evaluations has been clearly demonstrated in a variety of experimental studies. An especially persuasive one has the pointed title, "Liberal Grading Improves Evaluations but Not Performance.[14] Unquestionably, some instructors who receive unflattering evaluations deserve them. But other instructors are victims of their unyielding commitments to tough course requirements, demanding examinations, rigorous grading practices, or unfashionable intellectual positions. Because student evaluations cannot be relied on to distinguish such conscientious faculty members from their unworthy colleagues, dependence on these evaluations not only distorts the proper relationship between teacher and student but also menaces academic standards.

Granted, some educational researchers have concluded that student evaluations, viewed in proper perspective, can provide useful information. But the crucial insight, supported in hundreds of studies, is that student evaluations always need to be considered in the context of peer evaluations. Otherwise, as one researcher puts it, institutions are "flying blind."[15]

Corporate executives judge other corporate executives to decide promotions in the company, and attorneys judge other attorneys to decide partnerships in the law firm. Likewise, teachers should judge other teachers to decide matters such as reappointment, promotion, and tenure. Indeed, no professionals should shirk the responsibility of judging their colleagues. To do so is not only inappropriate but inimical to the interests of those supposed to be served. After all, if a quack is practicing surgery in a hospital, who is to blame, the patients or other physicians? If an incompetent is lecturing at a university, the ones at fault are not the students but the other professors.

Faculties rightfully claim authority in the academic sphere. When the time comes for evaluating teaching, they should not abandon that claim.

〜

CHAPTER THREE

Scholarship and Service

The Morality of Scholarship

Thus far I have considered faculty members primarily as classroom instructors. But in addition to teaching, most professors conduct research. Are they, in fact, obliged to do both?

If "research" is taken to mean continued study of one's subject, then the answer is affirmative. One entrusted with guiding others has the responsibility to stay well-informed. In an intellectual discipline, that commitment involves keeping abreast of developments as reported or discussed in scholarly books and journals.

When we seek legal counsel, we have a right to expect that our attorney is knowledgeable about recent court decisions and does not rely solely on cases studied during law school. Analogously, students are entitled to assume that their instructor does not merely repeat stale ideas, but is able to provide an informed account of the most promising lines of recent thought. A Ph.D. signifies that, as of the date awarded, the recipient has mastered a discipline. The degree does not grant the bearer a lifetime exemption from scholarship. A professor who depends on tattered, yellow notes reflecting timeworn thinking is as guilty of malpractice as the physician who relies on antiquated treatments. Both are ideal candidates for early retirement.

While faculty members are obligated to keep up with their fields, need they also make original contributions? For those whose teaching is confined to the introductory level and who would typically hold appointments at two-year colleges, a requirement to publish is not justified on pedagogical grounds. Someone can be a superb teacher of calculus without having authored papers in the frontier of mathematics. A similar point can be made, *mutatis mutandis*, about those who specialize in teaching introductory foreign language, English composition, or other such courses. Indeed, a doctoral degree need not be a prerequisite for handling these assignments. Teaching prowess, along with up-to-date knowledge of the subject and the methodologies for presenting it, should suffice. In contrast, most members of a four-year college or university faculty are expected to be able to work with students at any level, including those enrolled in specialized courses, advanced seminars, or independent study. In the case of these professors, the writing of books or articles relates directly to their pedagogic responsibilities.

Such activity helps hone skills in formulating creative ideas with care and precision. Not every notion that sounds convincing in conversation can survive the scrutiny endured by the written word, especially when the readers are experts. Those instructors expected to provide original perspectives in the classroom ought to have their abilities to do so evaluated periodically in accordance with rigorous standards set and maintained by peers who referee manuscripts for publication and comment on materials when they appear. For scholars to submit their work for such review is the equivalent of pilots undergoing periodic testing. In both cases, professionals are examined to determine whether their skills remain at the level necessary for the proper fulfillment of their duties.

All faculty members capable of conducting research are obligated to do so for yet another reason. Professors profess the worth of their subjects, and no subject can thrive in the absence of original contributions. No one is better qualified than professors to provide such sustaining creativity. Publications, then, ought to result from a faculty member's commitment to the advance of a discipline.

Even so, few contributors will produce revolutionary breakthroughs, and most can make only modest advances. But if the intellectual life is to thrive, numerous scholars must contribute to its growth. Even those blessed with genius build on the work of predecessors, weigh the comments of colleagues, and bequeath to successors the task of tracing the consequences of momentous insights. Therefore, faculty members able to contribute should heed the injunction of an ancient Hebrew sage: "It is not your duty to complete the task, but you are not free to desist from it."[1]

Once we recognize the value of scholarship, we should consider certain moral issues inherent in the endeavor. Whatever the specific methods of inquiry employed in a particular field, all scholars are bound by common ethical principles. Chief among these is the axiom that individuals should not claim credit for work they have not done. This rule prohibits all forms of plagiarism, including the use of unpublished materials obtained without consent from colleagues. Nor is it proper to appropriate ideas from students and pass them off as one's own. Acknowledgment is due any person who has contributed substantially to published work.

A corollary is that scholars should not have their names listed as co-authors of works actually written by others. This practice, while customary in certain fields, is blatantly dishonest. My work is mine, yours is yours, and mine doesn't become yours even if you are a senior member of my department with political clout. Several world-renowned scientists have been humiliated when articles bearing their names as co-authors were found to contain falsified data. Perhaps they had allowed themselves to become identified with the material as a favor to colleagues seeking to increase its visibility. Whatever the reason, if these luminaries did not contribute to the work reported, their names did not belong on those articles.

Another principle of responsible scholarship is that work should be carried out conscientiously, with due attention to detail. Otherwise the results will be unreliable and not a worthy contribution to the field. Thus available literature should be studied carefully, all citations should be accurate, opposing views should not be distorted, and conclusions should not be overstated. In addition, results should be presented in as useful a form as possible. The rule is violated by those who rush headlong into print as well as by those who permit themselves endless delays in completing their projects.

The former are so eager to accumulate credits that they do not take time to ensure that ideas are explained in a clear, orderly manner. Instead they produce a confused account which they expect their readers to unscramble. On occasion, editorial boards agree to publish such material on the grounds that it manages to convey significant thoughts, but they may be as dismayed as the eventual readers that the author has failed to prepare the manuscript with professional care.

Those who publish too quickly are often also guilty of publishing too much. The drive for quantity instead of quality succeeds in creating clutter, making it difficult to assess the significance of the author's contributions.

I remember one former colleague who published compulsively. He once invited several of us to browse through a six-feet-high metal cabinet filled with reprints of his innumerable articles, but in doing so we discovered that he had published the identical manuscript in two journals. When we inquired about this oddity, he replied self-consciously that he had submitted the article to one journal, forgotten about it, then submitted it to another. When he received two acceptance letters, he had been unwilling to forego a publication and so had not informed either journal of his error. Here was a fellow who clearly needed to think more and publish less.

Others exhibit the contrary failing. Whether from laziness, timidity, or a hopeless quest for perfection, they publish virtually nothing, receiving no feedback from peers and making no substantial contribution to progress in their fields.

This failing is exemplified by a man whom I first met when he was completing his doctoral dissertation, a comparative study of major movements in twentieth-century philosophy. The manuscript was apparently of such high quality that several professors at his graduate school urged him to consider submitting it for publication as his first book, an initial step on what they envisioned as a distinguished scholarly career. He assured them he would send it to a university press just as soon as it was polished, a promise he also made to colleagues at the college where he was appointed an assistant professor.

As he continued to refine the manuscript, however, it eventually seemed to him dated, so he undertook additional research and added new material. Then he felt the enlarged version needed further polishing, and retreated again to that chore. This fruitless cycle continued year after year. His colleagues suggested he try to publish sections of his tome as journal articles, but he was unwilling to do so, insisting that it appear only in its totality. Based on his continuing promise that the manuscript would soon be completed, he received tenure and a promotion. Almost twenty years have now passed, and he has not published a word of this work or any other.

Are his ideas of worth? He does not know, for he has not been willing to test them against professional standards. Would his work be a significant contribution to the field? We can only guess, for his peers have not been given the opportunity to read what he has to say. This man has thus done a disservice to himself and the subject he values. He has, in short, failed to fulfill his obligation as a scholar.

The Community of Scholars

While solitude may stimulate creativity, scholars do not flourish in isolation. They depend on publishers, librarians, research associates, and, most important, one another. How inappropriate, then, is the attitude displayed by those faculty members who view scholarship primarily as a path to self-aggrandizement. They delight in displaying their own erudition while dismissing the efforts of others. What these professorial peacocks fail to realize is that they are members of a community of scholars, without which they would be lost. If their colleagues did not provide the scholarly underpinning for the activities of university presses, specialized journals, professional associations, and institutions of higher education, what would remain of academic glory?

Too few scholars treat one another as though they were engaged in a cooperative enterprise. For instance, at a recent convention of the American Philosophical Association I met one of our country's most renowned philosophers, a man who had just published a remarkable book that was the talk of the profession. I told him how much I admired his newest work, then apologized for repeating what he had surely heard many times before. To my surprise he replied ruefully that, in fact, I was the first person at the meetings to have complimented him. Others had sought him out, but only to express disagreements; not a word of appreciation or encouragement had passed their lips.

Such failure to view other scholars empathetically is also apparent in the many book reviews that focus almost exclusively on a work's perceived weaknesses while saying little, if anything, about its possible strengths. One such review I read concerned a book in the history of mathematics, which, according to a footnote in the review, had been adopted as the chief text in a graduate seminar offered by one of the country's most distinguished scholars in the field. Surely, then, the book must have had notable virtues. Yet throughout eight pages the reviewer offered hardly any words of praise, limiting himself to such mixed comments as "the last four chapters [were] better argued than the rest." If the work had so little to recommend it, why did it deserve such a lengthy review?

A reviewer is entitled to express negative judgments. The reader should also be provided with a straightforward account of the book's contents and a generous presentation of whatever may be its stylistic and substantive merits. After all, the author spent thousands of hours writing the book; the least one can do is approach it sympathetically.

Scholars provide a variety of such formal services for each other, thereby maintaining standards of excellence. They referee one another's manuscripts to decide their worthiness for publication; they assess one another's grant applications to determine their suitability for funding; they appraise one another's academic records to advise institutions on faculty appointments and promotions. In each such case the scholar called on to conduct the evaluation has obligations both to the individual whose work is being judged and to those who will be guided by that judgment.

A preliminary point is that anyone asked to serve as a referee should not accept the assignment if uncertain whether the task can be completed on time. To agree to evaluate a manuscript, then let it lie unread for months, is a disservice to both the author and those depending on the review. Barring emergencies, work should be completed as promised. Nor does having too many obligations justify lateness. While those who allow themselves to become overcommitted may be well-intentioned, their failure to fulfill promises is as blameworthy as the irresponsibility of those who will not assume their fair share of such collegial duties.

Evaluators are assumed to be impartial, and they should therefore be explicit regarding any personal or professional relationships they have had with those whose works they are being asked to review. It should be no secret if the evaluator and the person being evaluated have been departmental colleagues, co-authors of a book, dissertation advisor and advisee, friends of long standing, or even, as in one case I knew, husband and wife. Those who have requested the review may decide that a past or present relationship does not disqualify the evaluator, but they should be offered the opportunity to make that judgment in the light of all relevant information.

Reliable evaluators do not indulge in captious criticism or inordinate praise. They refuse to glorify mediocrity but recognize that what is imperfect may nevertheless be meritorious. They focus on the work to be judged and not on irrelevant factors such as the author's personality or political persuasion. In addition, they acknowledge their own intellectual predilections, admitting that not all their judgments would be shared by other reputable authorities. One musicologist may have a penchant for late romantic music, another an aversion to it, but in assessing a critical study of the tone poems of Richard Strauss neither reviewer ought to suggest that all scholars agree as to the merits of these works. Even a conceptual or methodological schism within a discipline should not prevent a reliable evaluator from reaching a negative judgment about the work of an ally or a positive judgment about the work of an opponent. One may reject Platonism yet admire Plato.

The temptation for scholars to succumb to partiality is especially strong when they are called on to fulfill the most familiar of a professor's collegial obligations: the writing of a letter of recommendation. What is a faculty member to do when confronted by a student or colleague of less than the highest caliber who seeks written support for gaining admission to another institution, winning a fellowship, or obtaining an academic position?

The wrong approach is to provide a deceitful letter that exaggerates positive traits while disregarding negative ones. Those who engage in such dishonesty may view themselves as merely doing someone a favor with an innocuous fib, but some gullible souls are apt to be duped by the letter, act in accordance with it, and then face the disappointing consequences. As a result of the deception, other applicants may lose out on a vital opportunity. All are victims not of a harmless joke, but of outright dishonesty, the betrayal of a scholar's trust.

Professors who consistently write misleading recommendations may eventually defeat themselves. I once read a most impressive letter from a well-known philosopher, who concluded her praise of a young candidate for an assistant professorship by noting that, "His work is so superb that I have come to think of him not as my student but as my colleague, and I can't recall ever saying that about anyone else." This peroration seemed splendid, until I discovered that this professor wrote exactly the same words about every one of her advanced students.

Sad to say, such irresponsibility sometimes continues for years without anyone becoming the wiser. The most inadequate professor I ever knew had been recommended for his teaching position by a scholar of international renown who routinely wrote sterling letters on behalf of all his students. I doubt he ever suspected that his panegyrics would lead to educational havoc.

Much has been written about the baneful effects of grade inflation, but equally harmful are the consequences of recommendation inflation, which is nowadays rampant. If all the testimonials are true, every applicant to graduate school displays exceptional promise for advanced study, every applicant for a research fellowship possesses the capacity to produce a major scholarly work, and every applicant for a faculty position will be an inspiring teacher, a productive scholar, and a valued participant in campus life. Apparently no candidate suffers from any of the weaknesses that beset those who read or write such letters.

My award for overstatement goes to the faculty member who, when recommending a colleague for a prestigious national fellowship, described him as manifesting "the comprehensiveness of a Hegel" and "the rigor of a Kant." Probably the only person in the history of the world who would fit this description is Aristotle, and he has no need of financial aid.

How refreshing it would be to read a letter that began: "This is a candid recommendation. As such, it necessarily contains criticism as well as praise. Please read it in the spirit in which it is written." Such an exordium might succeed in rendering the contents believable, and if the subjects of such letters were accurately described, the author's credibility would have been established.

In any case, responsible professors should at least make clear to anyone requesting a recommendation that it will have to be a fair evaluation, not a fulsome encomium. And those displeased with this arrangement should not be accommodated. Just as counterfeit bills destroy monetary standards and cause disorder in the economic community, so phony recommendations wreck academic standards and lead to babel in the community of scholars.

Departmental Obligations

The mission of a college or university department is to promote excellence in the study and teaching of an academic discipline. Because scholars are committed to the worth of these disciplines, each professor ought to be a willing contributor to the life of a department.

What specifically are a faculty member's chief departmental duties? One is to teach courses that meet the most pressing student needs. To see the implications of this principle, let us assume that an English professor hopes to offer an advanced seminar devoted to a detailed study of *Ulysses*. This semester, however, the department needs someone to offer a course required for the major, a survey of twentieth-century British literature. In this situation a responsible instructor opts to meet a curricular necessity rather than satisfy a personal preference. Without such altruism, a department cannot fulfill its obligation to provide students with an optimal course of study.

Another departmental duty is to offer students guidance in planning their academic programs. Such advising is often mishandled in one of two ways. Either faculty members treat the matter perfunctorily, blithely signing cards without providing students with the benefits of an in-depth discussion of their academic plans. Or, on the contrary, professors coerce students rather than advise them. Such was the approach of a classics instructor I knew who took pride in declaring that even though her college had no foreign language requirements, she would never approve the program of a student whose plans did not include study of a foreign language.

Such an abuse of authority is irresponsible, but so also is a policy of indifference. Students are entitled to academic counseling, and faculty members, as scholars, are in a position to provide it. To do so effectively they need to pay careful attention to what each student says, then respond thoughtfully, taking into account individual capabilities and concerns. Even though their most sensible advice may sometimes be ignored, departmental members should care enough to offer it.

An additional professional duty is to take on a share of the sundry, day-to-day tasks that are an inescapable part of departmental life. Failure to join in this work is unfair to colleagues, overburdening them and weakening that cooperative spirit on which the success of a department depends. Indeed, trouble is on the horizon when those who have been volunteering their services suddenly realize that, as a former colleague of mine once put it, "more people are in this boat than are rowing."

One mode of significant participation is service on departmental committees, and an especially important one is that devoted to planning the curriculum. Its responsibility is not only to develop a systematically structured set of courses for majors, but also to design offerings suitable for students who may not become specialists. For example, undergraduates concentrating in history deserve an opportunity to study physics without embarking on a sequence intended for future physicists. Whether suitable courses will be available depends in great part on decisions made by curriculum committees.

I have thus far concentrated on obligations common to all members of a department, but senior professors have special responsibilities to their junior colleagues, be they teaching assistants, instructors, or assistant professors. Just as attending physicians are expected to offer guidance to residents, so senior professors should provide less experienced faculty members with advice regarding scholarly work, teaching methods, and appropriate standards of professional conduct. Such support should include a willingness to read and comment on manuscripts, to identify appropriate journals and presses that might publish such work, to visit classes and offer tips for pedagogical improvement, to review and make suggestions about course syllabi and examinations, and to discuss specific issues that may arise regarding academic ethics.

Failure to offer such help is blameworthy, but worse still are the actions of those senior professors who treat their junior colleagues with aloofness or disdain. When courses are to be distributed or schedules arranged, these academic poohbahs typically monopolize the choice assignments, disregarding the detrimental effects on those faculty members thereby burdened with unusually arduous programs. Even within a supportive environment, a junior scholar may have difficulty taking the first steps toward establishing a publication record while simultaneously teaching new subject matter and, in so doing, trying to master the fundamental principles of sound pedagogy. In a hostile environment these pressures are apt to become overwhelming, leading to loss of confidence and an inability to function effectively. Senior professors should be seeking ways to alleviate this problem; they should not themselves be aggravating it.

One particular member of a department is obliged to play the leading role in maintaining an appropriate departmental ethos: the one who has accepted the honor and the onus of serving as departmental head. Can this single person make an appreciable difference for the better? Unquestionably, but the task calls for both fortitude and tact.

Consider the case of a junior faculty member I knew who always came to class a few minutes late. The head of his department heard about the habit, took him aside, and diplomatically explained that instructors owe it to their students to arrive on time and begin class promptly. The advice was gratefully accepted, and the problem disappeared.

Note that the departmental head managed to hear about the problem, a circumstance not unconnected to being an interested listener. The proper response was not simply to hope the problem would disappear but to take an appropriate step to resolve it. The necessary action was not a public reprimand that would have caused ill will but a polite, private conversation that might even have increased this teacher's confidence in the departmental head's judgment and trustworthiness. Most important, the latter cared about the issue and responded in such a manner as to make clear to this teacher the department's commitment to proper standards of professional conduct.

The harder issues to handle are those about which members of a department disagree. But a satisfactory resolution can frequently be achieved if a departmental head acts fairly, respecting the rights of every faculty member while insisting that all adhere to appropriate principles of professional ethics. In such a case, reason often triumphs over rancor. Why, then, are many departments filled with discord? No single answer suffices, for, to paraphrase the opening sentence of *Anna Karenina*, all happy departments are alike, but each unhappy department is unhappy in its own fashion.

In one, for instance, authoritarian rule leads to resentment and eventual rebellion, while in another infirm leadership results in anarchy. Some are beset by hostile factions engaged in a variety of personal, political, or scholarly disputes, Although the origins of such a battle may be shrouded in ancient history, the feud lives on and continues to divide the members.

In-fighting is nasty and a waste of everyone's time. Worse, in such struggles students are typically used as pawns, and their academic needs are virtually forgotten.

How different is life in a friendly department where colleagues who might disagree intellectually nevertheless provide mutual support, offer one another pedagogical advice, comment on one another's scholarly papers, and work together for the common good. In such an atmosphere, the welfare of students is treated as of prime importance, and they are able to pursue their studies without the detrimental effects of personal animosities among the faculty.

Trying to maintain such harmony is an obligation for every faculty member.

Requirements

Professors are members not only of departments but also of faculties. As such, what are their duties?

Obviously, in addition to serving on college or university committees, faculty members ought to attend faculty meetings. Yet at many schools these assemblies attract only a handful of participants. As a former dean of mine once quipped, the only quorum obtained at a faculty meeting is a majority of those present.

To walk into such a meeting and find oneself virtually alone is a disheartening lesson in faculty irresponsibility. One issue, though, never fails to attract a crowd: college-wide requirements. Let someone merely propose that all candidates for a B.A. degree be required to demonstrate competence in writing English, and a vitriolic debate will ensue. Yet exactly what is supposed to be amiss about the faculty of a liberal arts college requiring students to master particular knowledge or skills?

Consider first an oft-stated objection to requirements that I heard again recently during a public discussion of a national report on education. One of the speakers, a university provost, criticized the report for its suggestion that all students would benefit from exposure to the humanities. The provost noted that such a view could lead in the direction of imposing requirements, a step, he warned, "incompatible with our goal of preparing students for a free society."

A free society, however, has not abolished all requirements. For example, every state in the Union has laws requiring any person who drives an automobile to have a license, pass a driving test, and obey the rules of the road. The claim that a driver is entitled to disregard red lights and speed limits lends support not to democracy but to anarchy.

Moreover, a free society imposes many requirements on its citizens, not the least of which is the requirement that each April we pay taxes to the government. Therefore it should not be incongruous or inappropriate for those learning to be thoughtful citizens to be required to study certain subjects. If the imposition of academic requirements presents a problem, it does not arise because of any conflict with our society's commitment to the Bill of Rights.

A far more serious objection to requirements centers on the concept of interest. Isn't an interested student easier to teach and likely to be a better student? A system of requirements fills classrooms with students who may have no interest in being there. Does it not follow that requirements are educationally unwise?

The virtue of this line of reasoning is that its premises are true. The argument's deficiency is that its conclusion does not follow from its premises.

While teaching interested students is easier, the aim of education is not to make life easy for professors. Presumably we find teaching talented students easier than teaching others. Nevertheless, we are obligated to teach all who enroll. Education is much more than merely preaching to the converted or hobnobbing with the elect.

Students arrive on campus with certain interests and needs. Unbeknownst to these students, however, their interests and needs may not match. Individuals may, in effect, be prisoners of their own immediate concerns, blindly pursuing what is narrow, shallow, or jejune to the detriment of their own personal and intellectual growth.

Many professors view a student's interests as sacrosanct. But these often develop haphazardly, without systematic exploration of available alternatives. What students happen to find intriguing at the time they choose their courses may be the result of suggestions from relatives or friends, the influences of the media, or the effects of good or bad teaching in elementary and secondary schools. Perhaps a family subscription to *Psychology Today* has sparked an interest in psychology, even though the student may not know the difference between psychology and philosophy. Perhaps a pamphlet from the check-out counter of a supermarket has convinced a student that the most relevant knowledge about the stars comes not from astronomy but astrology. Perhaps, to choose a more pointed example, a monomaniacal pre-med student is interested only in courses in the natural sciences, and believes work in the social sciences or humanities irrelevant to a physician's responsibilities.

Such cases could be multiplied endlessly. What they illustrate is that in a wholly elective system students may not choose their courses wisely and therefore may construct for themselves curricula that are either one-sided or muddled. Most faculty members are aware of this situation, but many are unconcerned, believing that if students select courses foolishly, the problem is theirs; they are, after all, adults who must live with the consequences of their own choices.

Here we arrive at the crux of the issue. Who is responsible for ensuring that a graduate of a liberal arts college has obtained the essentials of a liberal education? For those tempted to reply that the duty is the student's own, let me recall an event that occurs annually at college faculty meetings throughout the country. A ranking administrative official, usually a dean, rises and moves that the faculty approve as candidates for the B.A. degree those individuals on a list prepared by the registrar. Invariably, this motion is seconded and unanimously approved.

As a result of this faculty action, students on their graduation day receive an official document known as a "diploma," from the Latin word meaning "passport." It is, in effect, the student's passport to other educational institutions or various places of employment. The diploma states that its holder has satisfactorily completed an appropriate course of study and consequently has been awarded the B.A. degree. Who declares that individuals have earned this honor? The individuals themselves? Do they sign their own diplomas? If they did, such documents would be worthless. A diploma is granted on the authority of the faculty, and in virtue of that authority the worth of a diploma is recognized outside the college. If you sign a document attesting to some claim, you have the responsibility to ensure that the claim is accurate. Thus the faculty is responsible for ensuring that students granted B.A. degrees have, in fact, obtained the essentials of a liberal education. A faculty that cannot offer such a guarantee ought not to be issuing diplomas.

To view the matter from another perspective, consider a physician asked to sign a document attesting to your good health. The responsible physician does not do so unless satisfied that you pass appropriate tests. Suppose you request a physician to certify that you are in good health but to do so without examining your heart. You say to the doctor, "Don't bother with my heart. If it's not in good shape, I'll be the one to suffer. I'm an adult and can live with the consequences of my own choices." Any physician worthy of the name will reply that if you don't wish to have your heart examined, then you should go elsewhere to obtain a certificate of good health. If you insist on deciding which procedures are part of the physical examination, you might as well sign your own health certificate. If you wish to have the doctor's signature, the doctor ought to determine how the examination is to be conducted. A physician who signs health certificates without carrying out appropriate tests is irresponsible. The same should be said about a faculty that authorizes B.A. degrees without concern as to whether recipients have obtained the essentials of a liberal education.

In the face of this reasoning, some faculty members uncomfortable with the idea of requirements argue instead for instituting an advisory system. Their view is that students benefit when college-wide requirements are replaced by individualized guidance from an advisor. Is this approach satisfactory?

Consider the following familiar scenario. A student wishes to register only for courses in the humanities and social sciences. An advisor urges the student to take some work in the physical sciences, but the student balks. What to do? Different advisory systems offer different solutions to this common problem, but in the end every possible alternative involves either unfairness, faculty irresponsibility, or the implicit reintroduction of requirements.

Suppose students are permitted to disregard the recommendations of their advisors. In that case the faculty will be committed to the irresponsible action of awarding B.A. degrees to students who have not acquired the essentials of a liberal education. Suppose, on the other hand, that students are forced to adhere to rules laid down by the so-called advisors. Would students be subject to the same rules if they were to switch advisors? If different advisors are empowered to lay down different rules, then the system is unfair, because one student might have no choice but to study a laboratory science in order to obtain a degree, while another student might be permitted to substitute a course in science fiction. Suppose the rules for advisors are made uniform, so that for students to seek a new advisor to obtain a less stringent program is pointless. In that case we have, in effect, abandoned the advisory system and replaced it with a set of requirements.

One curious feature of the debate over requirements is that even the strongest advocates of a free elective or advisory system believe that requirements are appropriate within departmental majors. I have yet to hear anyone argue that a mathematics department need not require majors to learn calculus or that a music department need not require majors to learn harmony. Why are such requirements not considered oppressive?

A standard reply is that no student is forced to specialize in any field, but once that choice is made, the essentials of the subject should be learned properly. Similarly, no student is forced to choose a course of study leading to the B.A. degree, but once the choice is made, the essentials of a liberal education should be learned properly.

What are the essentials of this education that is supposed to provide a basic, systematic understanding of the world in which we live? I believe that if we were to poll faculty members of liberal arts colleges, most would subscribe to Sidney Hook's statement:

The answer to the question "What should we teach?" is selected materials from the fields of mathematics and the natural sciences, social studies, including history; language and literature; philosophy and logic; art and music. The knowledge imparted by such study should be acquired in such a way as to strengthen the skills of reading and writing, of thinking and imaginative interpretation, of criticism and evaluation.[2]

Disagreement arises when we seek answers to two questions. First, what specific requirements should be established for the B. A. degree? Second, what is the justification for encouraging large numbers of students to pursue a liberal education?

To answer the first question, no single set of immutable requirements is ideal for every liberal arts college; different schools have different resources as well as different priorities. Furthermore, any curricular decisions need to be reexamined constantly in the light of changing social and intellectual conditions. The crucial point, however, is that a faculty should be committed to structuring sensible requirements that embody the essence of a liberal education. Without these the faculty cannot reasonably decide whether students have earned liberal arts degrees, in which case the school's diplomas are a sham.

The second query is apt to bedevil any faculty meeting where the issue of requirements is raised. The pattern of debate at such a meeting is all too predictable. The head of the school's curriculum committee introduces a motion to the effect that all students be required to study a laboratory science, a foreign language, or perhaps the history of Western civilization. Regardless of the specific content of the motion, one sincere soul soon takes the floor to deliver a rambling speech that concludes resignedly with the rhetorical question, "But who here can actually tell us why all our students need a liberal education?" The meeting then turns into chaos, as the original motion is buried under an avalanche of amendments to the motion, substitute motions, and amendments to the substitute motions. Hours later, when exhaustion has set in, a survivor of the marathon session moves to table the entire matter. Amid sighs of relief this motion passes (thankfully it is undebatable), the meeting is adjourned, faculty members stagger out of the auditorium, and on each succeeding graduation day students receive their diplomas without having had to demonstrate any knowledge of a laboratory science, a foreign language, or the history of Western civilization.

Let us return to that critical moment at our hypothetical meeting when the faculty is challenged to justify liberal education, and try to formulate a concise and cogent reply.

Some would argue that liberal education is the study of subjects of intrinsic rather than instrumental value, to be learned for their own sake, not as means to some ends beyond themselves. To cite one proponent of this view, liberal education is "beyond utility."[3] Those who embrace this position are apt to speak longingly of the trivium and quadrivium, while expressing far less concern about recent developments in the physical sciences and social sciences. To their eyes the curriculum is a museum in which the wisdom of the past is enclosed and displayed, impervious to contamination from the laboratory and free of grime from the marketplace. In the words of Eva T. H. Brann, the instructor at St. John's College whom I just quoted, "Our time is not an era in which the scene of learning can teem with much newness. . . . That possibility began to vanish three centuries ago. . . . We are so situated as to be capable of no other novelty . . . than renovation."[4]

Even those who do not share such antiquarianism may believe that the content of a liberal education is self-justifying. The fundamental flaw in this approach was exposed long ago by John Dewey. Consider this comparatively neglected passage from his masterpiece *Democracy and Education*:

> We cannot establish a hierarchy of values among studies. In so far as any study . . . marks a characteristic enrichment of life, its worth is intrinsic. . . . Those responsible for planning and teaching the course of study should have grounds for thinking that the studies and topics included furnish both direct increments to the enriching of lives of the pupils and also materials which they can put to use in other concerns of direct interest.[5]

In other words, to argue that the content of liberal education is of intrinsic value and hence self-justifying provides no defense against the counterclaim that some alternative curriculum is also of intrinsic value and hence also self-justifying. If those who introduce a motion to institute requirements can defend their proposal only by claiming that the subjects they propose to require are self-justifying, no wonder faculty meetings turn into chaos. Pious sentiments are no substitute for a direct answer to this critical question: "What does a liberal education offer compared to other possibilities?"

Some respond by appealing to such notions as self-fulfillment, self-actualization, self-cultivation, or self-realization. The suggestion is that liberal education provides the most effective means of achieving these personal goals.

This approach faces serious difficulties. First, the ends themselves are vague; it is hard to explicate any of them or provide an account of how each differs from the others. Such terms are reminiscent of the old saying that liberal education develops "the whole person," an empty slogan that fails to explain, for example, how any individual can excel both as concert pianist and karate champion. Another problem is that however terms such as "self-actualization" and "self-realization" are understood, Garry Kasparov achieved this goal by playing chess, Jascha Heifetz by playing the violin, and Diana Taurasi by playing basketball. Yet none of these activities is central to anyone's concept of a liberal education. On the other hand, a significant number of those who complete a liberal education do not appear to be especially self-realized or self-fulfilled; to the contrary, they are sometimes discontented, disaffected, even disoriented.

A more promising defense of liberal education emphasizes the usefulness of acquiring a basic understanding of our world. After all, studying the physical sciences, social sciences, and humanities helps us make sense of the human condition.

A difficulty with this line of argument, however, is that it fails to demonstrate why a liberal education is significant to those who may lack the fervor to embark on a four-year quest for pure knowledge. In John Herman Randall's classic book on Aristotle, Randall cites Aristotle as one of a very small band of great "Knowers" in the Western tradition; the others he includes in this exclusive group are Spinoza, Hegel, and perhaps Thomas Aquinas.[6] We cannot reasonably expect that any of our students will eventually join the pantheon of great "Knowers"; indeed, only a comparative few are likely to make any important contribution to the sum of human knowledge. Nevertheless, our society commits enormous amounts of time and money to support institutions that offer a liberal education. Is this entire enterprise to be justified as a glorious effort to enable millions to sip from the font of pure wisdom? In that case, prudence might dictate that in light of our society's limited resources, we ought to provide a liberal education only to potential intellectuals, while furnishing all others just limited job training. Even if one rejects this policy as inconsistent with our country's commitment to equality of opportunity, the crucial issue remains: Why should all of us be expected to join what Randall calls "the passionate search for passionless truth"?[7] To be more specific, why require a future lawyer to study music, a future musician to study chemistry, a future chemist to study anthropology?

Some proponents of liberal education respond by observing that the most useful preparation for any career is not narrow job training. They argue persuasively that the concept of vocational education should be broadened to include the study of those scientific, historical, and ethical questions that illuminate any particular occupational path.

This reply is effective as far as it goes, but does not demonstrate why an individual ought to study all the essentials of a liberal education; rather, the response proves why an individual ought to study those specific aspects of a liberal education that happen to shed light on the person's chosen vocation. Consider again the case of the future musician asked to study chemistry. Granted that such an individual might be well advised to study subjects such as philosophy of art, French, German, or Italian, and even that branch of physics dealing with acoustics. But why chemistry? Why biology? Why physics, apart from acoustics? Indeed, why any subject whose connection to music is remote? A working musician might find some use for a knowledge of chemistry, but the mere possibility of such a situation hardly justifies a requirement that a future musician study chemistry. Any item of knowledge may be handy at some time, but that consideration does not call for an infinite list of requirements. In short, to defend liberal education as a component of vocational education fails to demonstrate why the essentials of liberal education are valuable for every student, regardless of future occupation.

The four justifications for liberal education that I have examined all suffer from the same flaw: each attempts to rest the case for a uniform course of study on factors that differ from person to person. Each of us finds a different set of subjects to be intrinsically valuable, each of us treads a different path toward "self-realization," each of us seeks to acquire different sorts of knowledge, and each of us pursues different vocational goals. How can such differences provide the basis for a common curriculum?

I propose that instead of concentrating on our differences, we ought to focus on our commonalities. In particular, we ought to take seriously our common responsibilities as free persons in a free society. Each of us is not only, for example, a lawyer, a musician, or a chemist; each of us is also a citizen. And, as stated previously, the welfare of a democratic community depends in great part on the understanding and capability of its citizenry. The justification for as many persons as possible to receive a liberal education is that it provides the knowledge, skills, and values all of us need to make a success of our experiment in self-government.

In addition to possessing an understanding of the democratic system itself, every member of a democracy should be able to read, write, and speak effectively so as to be able to participate fully in the free exchange of ideas so vital to an open society. Every member of a democracy should also be able to comprehend the range of public issues, from poverty, overpopulation, climate change, and ideological conflict to the dangers of nuclear warfare and the possible benefits of space research. These topics cannot be intelligently discussed by those ignorant of the physical structure of the world, the forces that shape society, or the ideas and events that form the background of present crises. Every member of a democracy should possess substantial knowledge of physical science, social science, world history, and national history.

The study of science assumes familiarity with the fundamental concepts and techniques of mathematics, because such notions play a critical role in the physical sciences and an ever-increasing role in the social sciences. Furthermore, to know only the results of scientific and historical investigations is not sufficient; one needs also to understand the methods of inquiry that have produced these results. No amount of knowledge brings intellectual sophistication, unless one also possesses the power of critical thinking. Every member of a democracy, therefore, should be familiar with the canons of logic and scientific method.

Still another characteristic that should be common to all members of a democracy is sensitivity to aesthetic experience. An appreciation of literature, art, and music enriches the imagination, refines the sensibilities, and provides increased awareness of the world in which we live. In a society of aesthetic illiterates not only the quality of art suffers but also the quality of life.

In connection with the study of literature, we should note that significant value is derived from reading a foreign literature in its original language. Not only does great literature lose some of its richness in translation, but learning another language increases linguistic sensitivity and makes one more conscious of the unique potentialities and limitations of any particular tongue. Such study is also a most effective means of widening cultural horizons, for understanding another language is a key to understanding another culture.

Every member of a democracy should also acquire intellectual perspective, the ability to scrutinize the fundamental principles of thought and action, encompassing both what is and what ought to be. The path to such wisdom lies in the study of those subtle analyses and grand visions that comprise philosophy. No other subject affords a stronger defense against intimidation by dogmatism while simultaneously providing a framework for the operation of intelligence.

Thus we have at last arrived at a powerful and persuasive reply that could have been offered to the bewildered professor at our hypothetical faculty meeting who asked, "Why do all our students need a liberal education?" Some wise, responsible, and courageous soul should have taken the floor and responded:

> I'll tell you why. A liberal education enables individuals to live intelligently and responsibly as citizens of our democracy. In view of the importance of this aim, every student awarded a B.A. degree should have demonstrated mastery of essential materials in the physical sciences, social sciences, and humanities. To ensure such mastery, I support the motion that we today institute an appropriate set of college-wide requirements.

A faculty that takes its obligations seriously would approve such a motion by acclamation.

~

CHAPTER FOUR

Personnel Decisions

Faculty Appointments

At many colleges and universities, the tradition holds that at the first faculty meeting of the academic year departmental heads introduce the new members of the faculty. Those presented have presumably been selected in accord with proper procedures. Exactly what steps should have been followed in order to justify a faculty appointment?

The process typically begins with a dean informing a department that it has been given the opportunity to fill a position. The members of the department then determine in which, if any, particular subfields candidates will be expected to specialize. This decision should reflect not partiality, but a disinterested assessment of the department's needs.

Such is not always the case. Too many departments are unbalanced, overemphasizing certain specialties while neglecting others of equal or greater importance. As a result faculty members may become parochial, while students are deprived of courses in significant areas of study. Granted, few departments can cover all specialties, but when the opportunity arises for a new appointment, attention ought to be given to overcoming weaknesses, not simply enhancing strengths.

Once the description of the position has been agreed on, a search should begin. Its aim is to find that candidate most likely to achieve excellence in fulfilling the varied responsibilities of a faculty member. Of course, every effort ought to be made to ensure that the search process is free of racial, religious, or sexual prejudice.[1] Also to be avoided is a rarely mentioned yet equally unacceptable form of bias: favoritism toward friends of departmental members.

The tendency is to overrate one's professional pals, then become angry if colleagues do not share this inflated view. To avoid the problem, all departmental members ought to agree before the search begins that no one is under any obligation to be favorably disposed toward anyone else's friend. All subsequent consideration of candidates should be untarnished by any reference to personal attachments.

To maximize the possibility that a search will be successful, the available position should be announced in whichever publications are most likely to be read by potential candidates. The announcement should be accurate, clear, and informative, stating explicitly whatever special criteria the department has decided to apply. Any such criterion not specified should not be used.[2]

The applications should be studied with care, not glanced through haphazardly. When the decision is made as to which candidates are to be interviewed, those no longer in the running ought to be so informed. The news will remove their uncertainty, which might otherwise persist pointlessly for months.

The first stage of the interview process usually occurs at a national convention, where members of a department meet perhaps ten to fifteen applicants, conversing with each for a half hour or more. This situation is demanding not only for those answering questions but also for those asking them. While interviewees may perform poorly, so may interviewers if they harass applicants, treat them inequitably, or make unwise choices from among them.

How can these mistakes be avoided? The most effective method is to ask all applicants the same basic questions, set in advance, and then write down the key points of each candidate's answers. Follow-up questions will differ in each interview, but by structuring all interviews alike and keeping a record of what was said, interviewers are protected against changing standards as the hours wear on, attention wanders, and one candidate begins to blur into another. Weeks later, when the candidates are evaluated at a departmental meeting or in discussion with a dean, the written record will prove an invaluable aid.

An additional benefit from asking prepared questions is that interviewers prone to badger candidates are to some extent restricted from doing so by the need to stick to the script. If they persist in unprofessional conduct, they should be taken aside by colleagues or the departmental head and told to cease and desist. An interview room should not become a torture chamber.

As to the questions asked, the most common error is to concentrate almost exclusively on the subject of the candidate's doctoral dissertation and ignore such matters as the candidate's range of interests, grasp of the details of diverse subfields, understanding of pedagogical problems, and commitment to high standards of professional conduct. The following questions would elicit such information:

> "Tell us something about your areas of interest outside the field of your dissertation."
> "Which specific issues in these other areas have you explored, and what recent literature devoted to these matters have you found most provocative?"
> "With regard to each of the courses you are prepared to teach, what topics would you cover, and which readings would you assign?"
> "What do you think of the practice of grading students, and how would you plan to approach this task?"

I would add one particular question that should be asked of every candidate, although it is rarely asked of any: "Tell us about your intellectual pursuits outside our own discipline." After all, a candidate is being considered for an appointment not only to a department, but also to an entire faculty. As such, the individual may be called on to participate in interdisciplinary programs, offer lectures on broad themes, or share in decisions affecting the entire curriculum. Some attention, therefore, should be paid to the range of a candidate's intellectual horizon.

Admittedly, an interview of broader scope may disconcert some applicants as well as their faculty sponsors. One of the latter complained to me that our department had been unfair to his student, because she had not been asked enough questions about her dissertation.

"Didn't you write us a letter about her dissertation?" I asked him.

"Certainly," he said.

"And you praised it highly," I added.

"Absolutely," he responded.

"Well," I said, "we believed you."

At the interview, hard questions should be asked and cogent answers expected. Those candidates who do not provide them should be eliminated from consideration, not out of animosity but from a firm commitment to maintaining excellence. The road to mediocrity or worse is littered with the excuses offered by department members for candidates whom they liked but who performed poorly in interviews. While an interview situation, like a musical audition, can be misleading, in both cases false notes signal trouble. Nervousness may cause a candidate to become inarticulate, but the more likely explanation is the candidate's own weakness in effective speaking. In any case, why presume nervousness will not reappear in a classroom? Interviewers, in short, should be kind and fair but not credulous.

After the initial interviews have been completed, the department decides on a short list of candidates to be invited for visits to the campus. These all-day interviews can be revealing, but the extent of their usefulness depends on the range of situations to which candidates are exposed. Too often a campus visit consists of little more than a scholarly presentation to the department's faculty, including a series of technical questions and answers, lunch with all interested members of the department, a quick chat with a dean, and farewells.

What should occur is quite different. Most important, each candidate should be asked not only to give a research paper but also to prepare a talk on an elementary topic, organized and presented as for introductory students. In this test of pedagogic skills, candidates should be judged by their handling of the four elements of sound instruction: motivation, organization, clarification, and generalization. I have heard numerous candidates offer such talks, and these presentations were invariably excellent predictors of success in the classroom.

Even so, few departments ask for a demonstration of teaching ability. Years ago, the head of the philosophy department at a large state university asked me whether at my school, like his, enrollment in phi-losophy courses had been shrinking. I told him that, on the contrary, it had been growing. He was amazed and wondered how I accounted for this phenomenon.

"Good teaching," I said. "We try to make sure that all the candidates we appoint have the capacity for both outstanding scholarship and outstanding teaching. What do you look for?"

"Just good scholars," he replied. "We wouldn't appoint anyone who hadn't delivered a scholarly paper to the department."

"Why not test their teaching, too?" I asked.

"Never thought of it," he muttered.

A campus interview should also include the candidate's meeting with instructors from other disciplines who have related interests. These faculty members can provide the candidate with a fuller sense of the school's academic resources and can also help the department evaluate the candidate as a potential contributor to the campus's over-all intellectual life.

Arrangements should also be made for a candidate to meet as many departmental members as possible, individually or in small groups. This approach increases the opportunity for candidates to gain famil-iarity with the department, as well as for the department members to form judgments about the candidates after in-depth discussion with them on a variety of topics. The narrower the range of contacts on which an evaluation of candidates is based, the less reliable that evaluation.

Note also that, at any stage of the interview process, candidates should not be asked certain sorts of questions, in particular those that have no bearing on performance as a faculty member and may raise doubts as to whether inappropriate criteria are being applied in the search process. For example, no candidate, regardless of gender, should be asked, "Will your spouse be living with you?" While clarify-ing when candidates are expected to be available for academic duties is entirely appropriate, how personal relationships will be arranged so as to fulfill obligations to the school is each candidate's own concern, not the department's. Similarly, no applicant, whether younger or older than average, should be asked, "Do you think you are the right age to assume this position?" Competence is an appropriate criterion for a faculty appointment; age is not, and to avoid misunderstanding it should never be mentioned.

After all the interviews are completed and, one hopes, have been conducted appropriately, the crucial decision remains: who is to be offered the position? In simple cases only one candidate has been unanimously judged outstanding. Frequently, however, one candidate excels on some criteria while another candidate excels on others, and disagreement persists about the weight to be assigned the different criteria. What then?

No easy solutions are possible and, sad to say, such deadlocks can create deep-seated ill will among formerly amicable departmental colleagues. But certain guidelines can prove helpful. First, all candidates should be judged as potential teachers, scholars, and contributors to the academic community. A poor prognosis for performance in any of these areas should normally be sufficient for disqualification.

Second, a candidate's personal traits should be considered relevant to the department's decision only if they are likely to affect the individual's performance as a faculty member. Thus if trustworthy sources indicate that a candidate is thoughtless, unreliable, or nasty, a concern for academic values dictates that this candidate not be appointed. But if the objections to a candidate focus on the individual's curious manner of dress or unusual living arrangement, then these matters should be disregarded, for they are not related to fulfilling the responsibilities of a faculty member.

A third suggestion for resolving disagreements about candidates is that while the relative importance to be assigned to teaching or research skills depends on the mission of the institution, the one factor that should not be subject to trade-off is a commitment to academic ethics. Any candidate who displays an insensitivity to such concerns should be eliminated from further consideration, regardless of other attributes. To appoint an irresponsible instructor is itself an act of irresponsibility.

If none of these considerations breaks the deadlock, after full discussion of the pros and cons of each candidate a vote will have to decide the matter. For the sake of tolerance, however, both those in the majority and those in the minority should realize that their judgments about the applicants are liable to change in the years ahead, especially with regard to the individual who receives the appointment. In one extreme case I recall, an individual joined a department with the support of all but two members. Several years later that department voted overwhelmingly not to renew his contract; only two members urged his reappointment, the pair who had originally opposed him.

Mistakes will occasionally occur, but human fallibility does not excuse improper procedures or thoughtless decisions that almost invariably lead to serious trouble.

Consider the case of one unfortunate departmental head who over the course of several years made half a dozen appointments, each one by his own later admission an egregious blunder. While he himself was a respected teacher and researcher, he naively supposed that an elaborate search process was a waste of time, that it was equally effective and far simpler just to appoint individuals who happened to come to his attention, perhaps because they were personal acquaintances of his departmental colleagues. Eventually he paid a high price for his lackadaisical approach. Those he had off-handedly chosen did not share his view that a faculty member should be reappointed only if active in research, and so they conspired against him, vilified his name across the campus, drove him from office, and turned the department into an academic imbroglio. The situation improved only after the arrival of a new departmental head and other new colleagues, all appointed under the supervision of a dean in accord with the strictest search procedures.

The lesson should be clear. Faculty appointments ought to be made with the greatest care. Professors who proceed otherwise are guilty of gross negligence, and they are endangering their students and themselves.

Tenure

Even those who know little about academic life are usually aware that senior professors hold tenure. Any reference to this prerogative invariably gives rise to the same questions: Why should anyone receive permanent job security? Does tenure not pamper the indolent and protect the incompetent?

Academic tenure is not as singular as often supposed. In most organizations of university size, employees, whether at lower ranks or in middle management, are rarely dismissed for cause. As a result of poor performance they may be passed over for promotion, given lateral transfers, or occasionally demoted, but hardly ever discharged. While plant closings or fiscal crises may precipitate worker layoffs, tenured professors, too, face the loss of their positions if a department is phased out or a school shuts its doors. We read of high-level business executives forced out of their offices, but the same fate may befall college or university administrators. The former typically cushion their falls with those lucrative compensations known as "golden parachutes"; the latter are usually able to find safety in professorial havens.

Even the mechanics of the tenure system are hardly unique. Consider large law firms, which routinely recruit new associates with the understanding that after several years they will either be offered permanent partnerships or required to depart. Colleges make similar arrangements with beginning faculty members.

Despite such analogies, however, undoubtedly tenure provides professors an unusual degree of latitude and security. They are privileged to explore any area of interest, to proceed in whatever manner they wish. No one may dictate to them that certain subjects are taboo, that certain methods of inquiry are illegitimate, that certain conclusions are unacceptable. Tenure thus guarantees academic freedom, without which inquiry may be stifled and its results rendered lifeless.

Can such freedom be preserved in other ways, perhaps by some form of multiyear contracts? The problem besetting any alternative scheme is that it could too easily be misused, subjecting faculty members to attack because of their heterodox opinions or unpopular judgments. For example, had the protection of tenure not been available to the departmental head I referred to at the end of the previous section, who made a series of unfortunate faculty appointments, his malicious junior colleagues would surely have driven this reputable scholar from the campus. As the historical record makes clear, such acts of intolerance produce an atmosphere of suspicion and recrimination, antithetical to independent thinking. Unquestionably the tenure system has dangers, but none is as great as those that would attend its abandonment. To adapt a remark about democracy offered by Winston Churchill, tenure may be the worst system ever devised, except for all the others.

To defend the tenure system in principle, however, is not to applaud the ways it has been implemented. Without doubt most colleges and universities have awarded tenure too liberally. Instead of individuals being required to demonstrate why they deserve tenure, a school has been expected to demonstrate why they don't. In court a person ought to be presumed innocent until found guilty, but in matters of special skill one should not be supposed competent until so proven. A school's failure to observe this guideline results in a faculty encumbered with deadwood, and more than a few departments suffer from this unfortunate phenomenon. To see how easily a mistake can be made, consider the following hypothetical but realistic case.

Adam comes to Eastern College to begin a professorial career. During his first two years he gains experience teaching standard departmental offerings while struggling with and finally finishing his dissertation, which he had optimistically estimated he would complete before his arrival. In his third and fourth years he devotes himself to planning several new courses and participating in an exciting interdisciplinary program. While reasonably successful as a teacher, he publishes two articles derived from his dissertation. In his fifth and sixth years he continues to enjoy good rapport with students while publishing a couple of book reviews and another article, this one based on a seminar paper written in graduate school. He has also begun work on what he hopes will be a book-length manuscript, but the project is still at an early stage.

At the end of six years, in accordance with the principles of the American Association of University Professors, Adam's tenure is decided. He is liked by his students, has various publications, and is at work on a major scholarly project. He is a cooperative colleague and has participated enthusiastically in interdepartmental activities. Should he be awarded tenure?

Doing so involves excessive risk, for Adam's most productive years may lie behind him. He has not demonstrated the capacity for sustained, creative effort, and a careful examination of his bibliography raises serious doubts whether he has produced any significant scholarship since his dissertation. His good rapport with students may be based more on a beginner's enthusiasm and spirit of camaraderie, possibly short-lived, rather than on fundamental pedagogic skills and enduring qualities of mind that would sustain his teaching in later years. Visits to his classroom may even have raised some doubts in this direction. His contributions to the life of the university may decline when the novelty of such activities wanes, and as time goes on he may not even keep in close touch with the frontiers of his own field. If he is awarded tenure, then fulfills our worst fears, those who suffer most will be the generations of students forced to endure his premature academic senility.

Of course, were he retained he might in the long run prove a significant asset to the university. But that outcome is only a possibility, not a probability. For the sake of future students as well as in the interest of each academic discipline, every effort should be made to appoint and retain only those individuals who, compared to all other available candidates, are most likely to achieve excellence. Adhering to such a rigorous standard is the surest way to avoid the succession of egregious and irremediable errors that are the inevitable consequences of laxity.

Adam's supporters, however, can be depended on to argue that in evaluating him we have placed too much emphasis on the criterion of publication. After all, they may remind us, one great teacher wrote nothing at all: Socrates. Those who appeal to his case tend to overlook that the Athenian gadfly spent his life in public debate, befuddling the cleverest minds of his day, and forcing them to rethink their fundamental commitments. No one would doubt the scholarly qualifications of any contemporary professor who could do the same. But, as Socrates himself pointed out, impressing students and friends is no guarantee of one's acumen.

Few who oppose the "publish or perish" principle would object to the demand that faculty members "think or perish"; yet to publish is to make available to all the results of one's best thinking. Professors who fail to do so must seek alternative ways of providing clear and substantial evidence of their intellectual vigor. If they are unable to shoulder the burden of proof, others are justified in doubting the quality of their thinking and, hence, their teaching.

Adam's supporters will claim that despite his thin publication record, he has proven himself a good teacher. But how good is he? Is he merely competent, or is he so outstanding that we have strong reason to suppose that by replacing him in the classroom we would significantly reduce the quality of instruction? Unless the latter were the case, we ought to appoint in his stead an individual who would at least match him as a teacher while surpassing him as a scholar. After all, why should a college award tenure to a present member of the faculty, if other persons more capable stand ready to serve?

In the face of this challenge, Adam's supporters are apt to retreat to the view that, while his credentials are admittedly borderline, we ought nevertheless give him the benefit of the doubt, taking into consideration the extra hours he has spent with students, the favors he has done for colleagues and, above all, the disturbance and distress a rejection could cause him. Those responsible for tenure decisions should never succumb to such pleadings; they are obliged to remember Sidney Hook's observation that "most . . . tenured faculty who have lapsed into apparent professional incompetence . . . were marginal cases when their original tenure status was being considered, and reasons other than their proficiency as scholars and teachers were given disproportionate weight."[3] The rule of thumb should be: when in doubt, say no. This policy will not be popular with Adam, his family, or his friends. But only by maintaining rigorous standards for the awarding of tenure can an institution safeguard its academic quality.

Not all difficult tenure cases conform to Adam's example. Suppose, for instance, Eve comes to Western University to begin her career. Her dissertation, completed prior to her arrival, is published by a leading university press. Throughout the next five years, she contributes a series of substantial articles to prestigious professional journals, and months before she is to be considered for tenure, her second book is accepted by a well-known commercial house. Unfortunately, her teaching record is less distinguished. Students often complain that her lectures are boring and bewildering and that she is rarely available for consultation outside class. Registration for her courses is small, although a few advanced students have signed up repeatedly. Visits to her introductory courses have revealed that she speaks in a monotone, while staring at the ceiling or peering out the window. Her presentations reflect a firm grasp of the most recent critical literature, but fail to motivate students and are unnecessarily convoluted. She has reluctantly agreed to serve on several departmental committees but is far more often seen in the library than in her office. Should she be awarded tenure?

The answer depends on the school's priorities. If the teaching of undergraduates is the primary mission of Western University, then Eve surely does not merit tenure. But if the university is devoted above all to the advancement of knowledge, and evidence strongly suggests that by replacing her, the faculty would significantly weaken its research effort, then she may deserve tenure. Her teaching, however, presents a serious problem. Perhaps she could work only with advanced students and not be placed in introductory courses. If she cannot be trusted to be effective at any level, then awarding her tenure is irresponsible, for even a university that places the highest premium on research is obligated to provide students with competent instruction.

Does Western University put equal weight on the advancement of knowledge and the teaching of undergraduates? Then the school needs to determine whether by replacing Eve the faculty could significantly strengthen its teaching and research. If a substitution could reasonably be expected to lead to such improvement, Eve should not receive tenure. If the issue is doubtful, the judgment should also be negative. Few individuals are indispensable, and a mistaken decision denying tenure is usually far less damaging to a school's well-being than a mistaken decision awarding it.

Note that had Adam excelled in teaching to the extent that Eve excelled in scholarship, their cases could have been analyzed along similar lines. If the advancement of knowledge were the primary mission of Eastern College, Adam would not have merited tenure. But if the teaching of undergraduates were the school's foremost priority, he might have warranted tenure, although his thin record of publications would still have been cause for concern. If the college put equal weight on research and undergraduate instruction, then the crucial question would have been whether by replacing him the faculty could have notably enhanced its combined efforts. If so, Adam ought not have received tenure.[4]

We should remember, however, that factors other than a faculty member's record as a teacher and scholar need to be weighed as part of a tenure decision. Service to the institution should be taken into account, especially if unusually meritorious. And of crucial importance is a faculty member's commitment to appropriate standards of academic ethics. A series of minor lapses from proper conduct should be counted negatively; major lapses should end consideration of tenure.

In short, much is at stake whenever any faculty member is awarded or denied tenure. Wise choices are a blessing, foolish ones a blight. Too many ill-advised decisions may bring tenure itself into disrepute, thereby threatening that academic freedom the system is intended to preserve.

Voting Procedures

Decisions regarding appointment, promotion, or tenure typically involve departmental voting. Who are the eligible voters, and should their individual judgments be kept secret? These procedural questions may appear of minor consequence, but they raise major issues of legitimacy and fairness.

Consider, for illustration, a department composed of nine members: three full professors, all tenured; three associate professors, only two tenured; and three untenured assistant professors. One of the assistant professors comes up for tenure. Who should vote?

Conflict of interest rules out all but the tenured members. Were those without tenure to participate, they would be voting on someone who might eventually vote on them. Two professors could exchange support for mutual advantage, or self-interest might lead each one to try to eliminate the other. In any case, considerations of personal advantage could too easily influence the voting, and the integrity of the process would thus be undermined. Similarly, if one of the tenured associate professors comes up for promotion, the only members voting should be the tenured full professors.

Suppose one of the assistant professors is considered not for tenure, but only for promotion. Should the untenured associate professor join in the voting? Again, conflict of interest prohibits such participation, for the status of all untenured professors is insecure, and because they themselves may be evaluated comparatively, considerations of job security can all too easily influence stated opinions.

Granted, no decision procedure can ensure the integrity of voters. At least we can avoid obvious situations where judges may lose or gain personal advantage as a result of their actions. For this same reason, when new departmental appointments are being decided, the voting should exclude untenured members. Their vulnerability to inappropriate influence, be it fear of a new rival or pressure from a tenured colleague, compromises the appearance and often the reality of their required independence.

Should students, the recipients of the education professors offer, be entitled to vote on personnel decisions? This question was raised, along with banners and fists, at colleges and universities throughout the country during the late 1960s, and to their shame numerous faculties sacrificed their autonomy in a misguided attempt to appease rampaging protestors. Students were given membership on faculty committees, encouraged to vote on matters of curriculum, and asked to make decisions regarding appointment, promotion, and tenure. Today at many institutions such privileges are accepted as a matter of course. Faculties have thus yielded their appropriate prerogatives to those who, by definition, lack the knowledge and experience essential to the legitimate exercise of academic authority. To sit in a departmental meeting and watch the vote of a self-assured freshman cancel out that of a distinguished professor is to be transported into the world of an Ionesco farce.

If students are not permitted to vote, won't their needs be disregarded? This oft-repeated, rhetorical question presumes that students know their own needs; yet, as Socrates emphasized, the good teacher leads students to an awareness of their own ignorance. Socrates, not his students, knew best what they needed. On occasion irresponsible faculty members may neglect the legitimate concerns of their students. So may irresponsible pilots endanger the lives of their passengers. Is the proper response to such malfeasance to ask the passengers to choose the pilots? Likewise, the answer to professorial misconduct does not lie in student suffrage. Such an infringement on the proper authority of the faculty exacerbates problems that can be resolved only by appropriate vigilance on the part of the professors themselves.

As to the claim that students have consumer rights, the point justifies complaints about a department's disregarding its own stated rules or an instructor's failing to teach standard materials. But consumers are not entitled to vote on who will serve as the management or staff of a company. If customers are dissatisfied with a firm's service, they are free to take their business elsewhere. Students have similar options in selecting instructors or choosing colleges.

Yet the consumer analogy is fundamentally flawed, for academic degrees are not purchased but earned. They represent the faculty's certification of an individual's academic achievement. If all students who paid tuition automatically received degrees, or if degrees were granted by vote of the student body, then diplomas would be meaningless. Awarding degrees is the faculty's prerogative, as is appointing qualified colleagues with whom to share responsibilities.

For students to exercise faculty authority also raises conflicts of interest. Obviously, students may gain or lose personal advantages from changes in curricular and degree requirements, and the professors they evaluate may in turn evaluate them. The entire situation is rife with potential abuses.

Should members of a department be given free rein in making personnel decisions? Because a professor is part of a faculty, sharing its privileges and subject to its regulations, that body should oversee matters of appointment, promotion, and tenure. This responsibility is most effectively fulfilled by an elected faculty committee constituted by representatives from the school's diverse intellectual areas. Its task is to examine the documentation submitted in support of departmental recommendations, to ensure both that proper procedures have been followed and that judgments have been adequately defended. Occasionally, these recommendations will have been distorted by partisanship, internecine feuding, or even raw prejudice; the committee's duty is to identify such cases and rectify the errors. Caution needs to be exercised, however, in overturning a department's judgment, for those within a discipline know it best and are most familiar with the performance of the individuals being evaluated. A faculty committee should follow the practice of a football referee after viewing instant replay: uphold close calls, but overturn flagrant errors.

When deciding on promotion or tenure, should the committee announce only the outcome of its deliberations, or should its reasons also be provided? Equally important, should the judgments of individual members be kept secret? These same questions apply equally at the departmental level.

Important considerations pull in opposing directions. After all, the need for candor from departmental colleagues and committee members suggests that to protect them against intimidation or retaliation, their individual votes and supporting arguments should not be divulged. An equally important consideration, however, is that the essence of a university is its open atmosphere of unrestricted inquiry, where claims are tested by public canons of reason and insights are shared in a spirit of cooperation. How inappropriate, then, are concealed evaluations, clandestine charges, and secret votes. Closed doors may encourage frankness, but they also shield narrow-mindedness, negligence, and sheer prejudice. In view of these telling points both for and against confidentiality, what procedures should be adopted?

As to departmental voting, yeas and nays are not sufficient. A candidate is entitled to the opportunity to respond to the arguments used by colleagues in arriving at their judgments, and the oversight committee of the whole faculty needs to assess the cases presented by both the department and the candidate. Thus each vote should be accompanied by a detailed statement of evaluation. This procedure is not only in accord with a university's commitment to the life of reason, but also discourages irresponsible faculty members from voting without having taken the time and effort to study the relevant evidence.

Some years ago I learned of a department that had opposed granting tenure to one of its members. This judgment was questioned by the oversight faculty committee. Thereupon the most distinguished member of the department announced that, in light of the committee's doubts, he had read the candidate's work and found it unimpressive, just as he had assumed it would be. This professor should already have studied these writings before voting on hearsay. Requiring faculty members to explain their votes discourages such dereliction of duty. The rule also forces those departmental members guilty of prejudice to rationalize their opinions, a disagreeable task that may serve to arouse a dormant conscience.

Should departmental decisions require a secret ballot? Because those voting will have worked with the candidate for a number of years, their judgments are apt to be predictable and their anonymous statements of evaluation easily identifiable. Furthermore, some voters are likely to be among the candidate's closest friends, and will have participated in meetings of the tenured members, where the candidate's strengths and weaknesses were openly discussed. In view of these circumstances, any attempt to build a wall of confidentiality is virtually bound to fail while almost sure to detract from goodwill, open discussion, and a spirit of cooperation.

Far more promising is the approach adopted in one department with which I am familiar, where members enjoy rapport while still holding each other to the highest standards of academic performance. When a personnel decision is made, those who voted take it upon themselves to meet individually with the candidate and explain the bases for their judgments. Sometimes they are forced to convey negative opinions, but their willingness to speak forthrightly rather than hiding behind an unenforceable code of secrecy contributes much to reinforcing the department's sense of collegiality and its shared commitment to the pursuit of excellence.

Even in a large department where such a personalized procedure may not be feasible, the principle of openness is equally applicable. After all, departmental voters enjoy the security of tenure. Seeking to provide them with the additional protection of confidentiality is not only impractical but also increases tensions and inhibits free exchange of opinion. In short, members of a department need to stand up and be counted.

Consider finally those who serve on a faculty oversight committee. They are volunteers, apt to avoid participation if their decisions expose them to personal attacks. Unlike voters at the departmental level, though, committee members have only limited contact with a candidate, thus making it more difficult for their individual judgments to be known beforehand and easier for their votes to be shielded after the fact. In sum, the overall situation favors confidentiality.

The committee, however, is obliged to communicate a justification for its decision, thereby demonstrating adherence to the rule of reason and affording the candidate an opportunity to prepare a response prior to final administrative action. Because those voting are less knowledgeable than the departmental faculty about the background of the case and the fine points of the discipline, their concerns will usually be of a more general sort, most appropriately conveyed not in a host of personal statements but in a majority and, if necessary, a minority report. In preparing this material committee members need to speak frankly with one another, as they can in closed session, assuming all are pledged not to reveal any of the proceedings. Incidentally, should anyone on the committee happen to be from the same department as the candidate, conflict of interest prohibits that member from participating in the case; otherwise, individuals would be deciding whether to sustain or overturn their own judgments.

In conclusion, while any of these practical guidelines may need to be modified in special circumstances, an appropriate balance always needs to be maintained between the protection secrecy affords and the danger it presents.

Faculty Dismissals

Virtually every college and university is burdened with at least one senior faculty member who displays flagrant ineptitude or irresponsibility. Tenure, properly understood, provides no protection for these guilty individuals. In fact, the American Association of University Professors' own "Statement of Principles on Academic Freedom and Tenure" envisions the possibility of "termination for cause" and describes a method for "the hearing of charges of incompetence."[5] Why, then, do tenured professors so rarely lose their positions?

Faculty members are understandably loath to brand colleagues as unfit, publicly disgracing them and, in effect, forcing them out of the profession. Furthermore, conducting appropriate procedures involves an enormous amount of time, trouble, and expense, especially considering the endless appeals certain to ensue. Because neither judges nor juries are experts in the relevant subject areas, proving inadequacy is no easy matter.

Yet these considerations ought not be allowed to render instructors immune from dismissal. To tolerate gross misconduct is to make a mockery of morality. At the same time schools must preserve the crucial distinction between behavior that is unusual and that which is unacceptable. The call for competence should never be interpreted as a demand for conformity. Where should lines be drawn?

No indulgence should be shown to faculty members who repeatedly and inexcusably miss their classes. I heard of a professor who decided in August that he would like to spend the next few months in Europe. He did not bother to share these plans with the members of his department but simply departed for Paris, leaving his colleagues to find a way to cover his scheduled courses. He deserved to be discharged; instead, his school, seeking to avoid a confrontation, issued him a toothless warning.

Equally blameworthy are those instructors who come to class but invariably ignore all their other pedagogical responsibilities: failing to appear for scheduled appointments, not bothering to return papers, not caring enough to submit grades. No appeal to the charms of eccentricity can justify such wholesale neglect.

Other strong candidates for dismissal are those professors who regularly misuse class time by not presenting the announced course material but, instead, engaging in self-indulgent ramblings or ideological harangues. For example, a professor of my acquaintance who is assigned to teach nineteenth-century philosophy regularly inflicts on his students lengthy tales about the history of his own department, denouncing colleagues for their alleged past and present wrongs. Sad to say, he has continued this misconduct for more than a decade without counteraction by his university.

As to the despicable practice of exchanging academic favors for sexual ones, should there be any confirmed instance of such an offer, the guilty professor should be sent packing. Blackmail has no place on a college campus.

Nor does fraud. When faculty members announce experimental findings, the data are supposed to be authentic. When faculty members quote primary sources, the citations are expected to be accurate. When faculty members submit curricula vitae, the information is presumed to be factual. Should any professor intentionally violate such trust, that individual forfeits the right to an academic position. The intellectually dishonest ought not be entrusted to lead the search for truth.

Fortunately, instances of deceit are rare. Not uncommon, however, are cases of sheer inadequacy. Why would a faculty member who has been awarded tenure suddenly begin to show signs of incompetence? The reasons vary: some saddening, some irritating. One professor may suffer from alcoholism; another may be consumed by debauchery. One I knew inherited a fortune and soon lost interest in academic pursuits.

Others may fall victim to their own laziness, failing to keep abreast of developments in their disciplines and eventually succumbing to scholarly obsolescence.

Such cases occur rarely. Yet they make clear the importance of schools not only bringing immediate charges against any faculty members deemed guilty of outrageous behavior but also establishing procedures to review regularly the work of all tenured professors. The absence of such safeguards is no tribute to academic freedom but an invitation to academic irresponsibility.

Implementing an effective system for identifying faculty members who perform unsatisfactorily need not be excessively complicated. As part of processing sabbatical applications, most schools evaluate at seven-year intervals the work of tenured professors. The department assesses an individual's research, judges its quality, and recommends to a faculty oversight committee whether the institution should support that person's leave. Why not expand these periodic reviews to include all senior faculty members, considering not only their contributions to scholarship but also their effectiveness in teaching?

Minimal levels of fitness, like standards for awarding tenure, will vary depending on an institution's mission. The competence of a professor of English at a graduate school should be judged differently than the competence of a specialist in expository writing at an undergraduate college. In all cases, however, the priorities of a specific school and the responsibilities of a particular position will imply appropriate criteria for acceptable performance.

In establishing the adequacy of a faculty member's research, the clearest proof is provided by scholarly publications. In their absence, unpublished writings can be reviewed by outside evaluators. Should no materials be available, individuals being evaluated should be expected to offer persuasive evidence that they have continued to conduct research at an appropriate level.

To confirm the adequacy of a faculty member's teaching, the best evidence is provided by peer observers. If their visits raise significant doubts or fail to resolve serious student complaints that may have been communicated to the department informally or through grievance procedures, outside evaluators should be invited to the campus to attend the individual's classes and offer judgments. Those evaluators selected should be sympathetic to the instructor's intellectual perspective, thus minimizing the possibility that disciplinary disagreements will be confused with pedagogic criticisms.

When a departmental decision is reached questioning a professor's adequacy, a recommendation should be forwarded to a faculty oversight committee, which is entitled to request additional information, including further outside evaluations. If after due deliberation the committee chooses to charge a faculty member with incompetence, the matter should then be brought to an elected faculty hearing committee whose primary responsibility is to judge such cases. Proceedings should be held at which the instructor is permitted to have counsel as well as to call and cross-examine witnesses. Most important, the burden of proof to establish adequate cause for dismissal should rest on the institution, not the individual, and should be satisfied only by evidence that is clear and compelling.

These strict procedures, which are in accord with regulations approved by the American Association of University Professors,[6] should serve to protect all tenured professors whose unpopular views or odd habits may lead bigots to call for their dismissal. Such intolerance is antithetical to the ideal of a university, which is committed to harbor dissent, nonconformity, and even the most unpopular of heresies. What should not be accepted is professional malfeasance. The longer the guilty are permitted to thrive, the greater the shame of their derelict colleagues.

CHAPTER FIVE

~

Graduate Education

At which stage in the education of future faculty members ought they be imbued with the sense of a professor's responsibilities? In graduate school, certainly. And at which stage are future faculty members most likely to be subjected to neglect or mistreatment by their mentors? Unfortunately, the answer is the same. Instead of serving to clarify and emphasize faculty obligations, graduate education frequently backfires, resulting in these duties being misunderstood or denigrated. How might the situation be rectified?

Note first the crucial difference between graduate work and most other professional study. Students who enter law school, for instance, take a series of lecture courses and are required to pass examinations in each. The first year is the most arduous, the second considerably easier. The third hardly ever presents serious difficulties. Indeed, those students who after their first year accept invitations to serve on the law review usually find that during their second and third years they spend more and more time doing editorial work and less and less time preparing for class. Nevertheless their doing well enough in their courses to obtain degrees is a foregone conclusion.

Graduate students rarely enjoy such security, for they confront a succession of tasks that become not easier but increasingly more demanding. Consider the familiar pattern. During the first year or two, students attend various seminars, each calling for the writing of a term paper on a topic of choice. Grading is lenient; A's are at least as common as B's, C's quite rare, and students unable to finish papers on time receive incompletes.

While continuing to accumulate credits, students are aware that ahead of them stands the hurdle of comprehensive examinations (nowadays less common). These are not tied to specific courses but call for a firm grasp of an entire discipline. Although the faculty may provide extensive lists of suggested readings, students prepare for the tests independently. Grading is strict, and failures on two attempts normally result in forced exit from school.

Even when these examinations are passed, the most rigorous requirement remains: writing a dissertation. No matter how promising a student's previous academic record, the challenge of planning, researching, and composing a book-length manuscript offering a new perspective on a scholarly subject may prove insuperable. Fruitless months may be spent trying to formulate a suitable topic, one that is original but not eccentric, consequential but not Herculean. Assuming such a subject can be found, the research may prove frustrating. Critical documents may be unobtainable; important assumptions may turn out to be questionable; crucial experiments may prove inconclusive. Yet, presuming that all goes well, the effort to complete a manuscript of a couple of hundred pages or more can lead to paralysis. Under pressure to organize the results of thousands of hours of work into a coherent, innovative, narrative able to withstand the scrutiny of experts, students may find that their work stalls. In the meantime, years pass, and research becomes dated. Eventually the best of intentions may be permanently thwarted.

All these difficulties produce the familiar phenomenon of the "ABD," an ironic acronym that refers to an individual who completes All requirements for the doctoral degree But the Dissertation. Such an unsatisfactory outcome is a unique feature of graduate education. After all, students in law school do not spend three years and thousands of tuition dollars only to discover at the very end that degrees are unattainable. Graduate students, however, like marathon runners, may see the finish line just ahead yet collapse without reaching it.

Do members of graduate faculties recognize these special problems and try to alleviate them? One hopes so. Yet too often the professors themselves are part of the problem. Indeed, many former graduate students, years after leaving school, still maintain deep animosities against teachers who, rather than helping students, contributed to or took advantage of their plights. This phenomenon is not accidental, but a consequence of educational policies, common to most graduate schools, that leave students exposed to faculty whims, while allowing, even encouraging, such capriciousness.

Consider how departments decide the courses offerings. The procedure is often merely to invite individual professors to announce the topics of their choice. That conglomeration becomes the curriculum. The list may be unbalanced or of little use to students preparing for their careers, but such concerns are apt to be viewed as beside the point. The focus is not on meeting student needs but on satisfying faculty desires.

The quality of instruction is frequently disappointing. Professors too often presume that by teaching at an advanced level they have transcended the need to observe principles of good pedagogy. Thus motivation may be omitted as unnecessary, organization denigrated as prosaic, clarification spurned as simplistic, and generalization dismissed as unscholarly. No wonder graduate students find many of their classes dreary, bewildering, and disheartening.

Another problem is that professors are tempted to consider any graduate course, even an introductory one, primarily as an opportunity for developing their own research and enlisting supporters in the effort to work on its fine points. Such an approach may provide students with insights into recent scholarship but fails to offer what they need most: a thorough and balanced understanding of a discipline's fundamental methods and materials. Graduate students have been short-changed, when, as is all too common, they leave school believing that their professors' opinions dominate the field, only to discover later that competing views are at least as influential.

This egocentric style of graduate teaching is also flawed by suggesting to students that professional success depends on sharing their instructors' intellectual outlooks. Professors should not attempt to attract devoted bands of personal disciples; that goal is appropriate for gurus. Graduate faculty members should hope to foster a future generation of well-informed, independent-minded scholars, and courses should be conducted to achieve that aim.

An additional purpose a course should serve is to provide preliminary challenges that can help students judge their chances of completing the arduous path to a doctoral degree. Evaluations from teachers ought to be useful in making such determinations. Yet instructors often award inflated grades, thus leading students to overestimate their capabilities and commit substantial time, effort, and resources to a cause the professors recognize as virtually hopeless.

Why would faculty members engage in such deception? Like almost everyone else, they prefer to give good news rather than bad. They are reluctant to discourage any student who has even the slightest chance of success. Most important is the unfortunate practice, common to most graduate schools, of considering a C akin to failure. Instructors are thus forced to award B's to students who do minimally satisfactory work and A's to those whose performance is just a bit better. No wonder so many students believe their work excellent, only to be shocked when they fail subsequent challenges.

In colleges and most professional schools, C is supposed to denote a satisfactory level of performance. If graduate schools adhered to the same policy, then faculty members would have at their disposal a convenient symbol for identifying work that was adequate but not promising. Students could thereby be forewarned of impending difficulties. Surely this approach is far preferable to that recommended by one departmental head who, when asked to justify the extraordinarily high percentage of A's given by his department, replied confidently: "That's no problem. Our students always know when they don't do well. We make it obvious with an A−." Perhaps he was fooling himself, but surely he was fooling his students.

Grading procedures and the conduct of courses are clearly not the only areas of responsibility for graduate faculty members. Overseeing comprehensive examinations is another.

Preparing for these is such a daunting challenge that students periodically urge their abolishment, and faculty members may welcome the opportunity to avoid developing and grading these examinations, preferring to replace them with research papers. But in so doing faculty members fail to fulfill their obligation to ensure that those who receive doctoral degrees have mastered their fields. Comprehensive examinations are the one occasion when students are required to demonstrate a firm grasp of all the major areas within a discipline, an achievement that provides a sound framework for a lifetime of study.

Granted, the essence of doctoral work is specialization, but a scholar needs broad perspective, not tunnel vision. As the historian Jaroslav Pelikan noted, "The difference between good scholarship and great scholarship is, as often as not, the general preparation of the scholar in fields other than the field of specialization."[1] A sound liberal education supplemented by graduate courses in different fields will go a long way toward achieving breadth outside a discipline, but the most rigorous test of breadth within a discipline is the passing of comprehensive examinations. For that reason they should not be abandoned, especially not to appease student demands or lighten faculty responsibilities.

Obviously, these examinations should be constructed carefully and graded scrupulously. What may be overlooked, however, is the importance of limiting the materials for which students will be held responsible. The scope of an entire discipline is so vast that not even the most learned scholar controls it all. Pretending that graduate students can accomplish this feat is not only senseless but possibly malicious.

On which books or issues will questions focus? A list should be provided that may be long but not interminable. Making sample questions available is also helpful. The preparation of such materials takes effort, but the same faculty members who complain about having to spend time on this task will, when pursuing their own work, expect support from colleagues, research assistants, and secretaries. Only laziness or selfishness accounts for the reluctance of these professors to furnish their students with the guidance they deserve.

The most critical area of a graduate professor's responsibility is advising students on their doctoral dissertations. Here horror stories are legion. These include the typical tale of the advisor who saddles a student with a topic so difficult that it would take decades to complete; or the advisor who does not return a student's work for more than a year; or the advisor who, without making clear exactly what the problems are, insists that drafts be endlessly revised. Students subjected to such mistreatment are apt to become so filled with frustration, anger, and resentment that they find continuing their work impossible.

Consider, for example, the following scenario. You are seeking a Ph.D. in English and have completed all necessary courses and passed all comprehensive examinations. You wish to write a dissertation analyzing the works of the playwright Harold Pinter, but the department's only specialist in twentieth-century British literature does not believe Pinter an important enough figure to merit a dissertation. You argue your case, citing one authority after another in support of your view. But after several months of dispute the professor still does not yield, despite admitting, to your astonishment, that he has never read any of Pinter's plays. Exasperated, you approach another professor who, although specializing in American literature, is willing to serve as your advisor. You spend a year writing the dissertation, but then the first professor is appointed to your doctoral committee and demands that you expand your study to include a chapter comparing Pinter with Chekhov. Seeing no alternative, you take another three months to comply, but your nemesis judges your new chapter unsatisfactory and is unwilling to pass the dissertation unless your analysis of Chekhov is thoroughly rewritten and greatly expanded. Six months later, after you have met this demand, your work is deemed satisfactory, and you arrive at your dissertation defense. But there the two professors become embroiled in a heated argument about the merits of your approach to dramatic criticism, and the other members of the committee, not wishing to antagonize either disputant, vote neither to approve nor disapprove the dissertation, but to require major revisions, including a new introduction, a revised conclusion, and an additional chapter discussing the works of various playwrights who might have influenced Pinter. The committee agrees that the dissertation will be passed only after both contending professors approve the new material. When informed of this decision, your likely response will be sheer fury. The next day, after you have cooled off and had time to deliberate, the proper strategy will become clear: obtain application forms and enroll in law school.

I wish this story were apocryphal, but it is only an amalgamation of events that befell several students I knew well. Under such circumstances, is no recourse possible?

Departments should have in place a process for conducting hearings, whereby students who believe themselves aggrieved are afforded the opportunity to have their cases adjudicated. Determinations should be made by a committee of senior faculty members who, by prior understanding, are prepared to rule against any of their departmental colleagues, no matter how distinguished.

An additional safeguard should also be established: a university-wide faculty committee to consider appeals of departmental decisions. To those who might reject this idea on the grounds that the agenda of such a committee would be flooded, I reply that such a phenomenon would itself be the clearest evidence of the urgent need for such a committee.

Dissertation advisors can make or break careers. A student provided with sensible suggestions about choosing a topic, constructive criticism as the project proceeds, polite but insistent urging to finish, and encouragement throughout, should, working full time, be able to complete the dissertation in less than two years and possibly closer to one. Given an inept or irresponsible advisor, a student can become like Tantalus, condemned to watch the object of desire recede at every attempt to obtain it.

Thus far I have considered ways in which faculty members should guide graduate students toward their scholarly goals. But many of these students are planning careers not only as researchers, but also as teachers. Here is where graduate education has historically been grossly deficient. Most future professors spend no time whatever in formal study of the art of instruction. They are forced to learn on the job, with their students as guinea pigs. Indeed, while individuals who apply for faculty positions will, as proof of scholarly competence, typically hold doctoral degrees or their equivalent, these same applicants are not usually expected to offer any evidence of ability to teach. While a thorough grasp of subject matter is necessary for effective instruction, erudition does not guarantee classroom know-how. Where should essential pedagogical skills be acquired?

The most practical approach is for graduate schools to offer courses in methods of teaching and require them of all students who are to be recommended for faculty appointments. These courses should involve future professors in discussing and practicing all phases of the teaching process, including motivating students, choosing materials, presenting lectures, guiding discussions, constructing examinations, and grading papers. Emphasis should be placed on the crucial importance and multifaceted nature of a professor's ethical obligations. Those selected to direct such courses should themselves be skillful and conscientious instructors, for they should be not only talking about pedagogical excellence but also exhibiting it.

No program of study can turn poor teachers into great ones. But if introduced by distinguished mentors during those formative years when individuals are most likely to welcome suggestions, a course of study can turn inaudible lecturers into audible ones, disorganized seminar leaders into more organized ones, and careless graders into more careful ones. Most important, it can turn thoughtless instructors into thoughtful ones, the critical step on the path toward more effective and responsible teaching.[2]

In no educational setting other than graduate school are such extremes of both exemplary and egregious faculty conduct taken for granted. To illustrate the point, consider two final episodes, neither as unusual as one might suppose.

The first was told to me by an unimpeachable witness who was taking a course from a renowned scholar at one of the country's leading graduate schools. This professor had originally distributed a list of assigned readings for each week's session, but as the semester went on he fell further and further behind schedule. With three weeks remaining in the term, he stood before the class and explained the problem. "There's no way we're going to be able to finish all the books I had hoped we would." At this point the class expected him to shorten the list, but he had in mind a different solution. "Why don't we cancel the rest of the class meetings?" And so he did. The irony is that, given the quality of his teaching, no one objected.

How different are the experiences of those fortunate students who begin graduate work unsure of themselves and their plans but, thanks to the efforts of even one concerned teacher, leave school not only with a doctoral degree but with increased self-confidence and a sense of intellectual purpose. Many of my colleagues tell such stories of their years in graduate school, but I shall close by relating in detail the case I know best: my own.

When I enrolled as a graduate student in the Department of Philosophy at Columbia University, I was unsure that I was taking the right step. Indeed, I still wondered whether I ought instead to have been attending law school, embarking on a doctoral program in American history, or studying piano at a conservatory.

As I looked through that semester's offerings, I came upon a course titled "Philosophical Analysis." I had no idea what it was about and was unfamiliar with the instructor, but, taking a chance, I enrolled.

The next afternoon I entered the department's luxurious seminar room, sat down in one of the plush chairs, and, with about thirty other students, awaited the appearance of our professor. When he arrived, he began by telling us that this course would be different from others we might have taken. We would not study the writings of famous philosophers of the past or pore over learned commentaries about them. Rather, we would *do* philosophy. We would not read about philosophers; we would ourselves *be* philosophers. Having spent many undergraduate hours struggling with difficult-to-understand works written centuries ago, I welcomed whatever he had in mind.

He informed us that the reading for the course would consist only of a few articles, and that we would be writing three papers in which we ourselves tried to solve the very issues discussed in those articles. I found this proposal hard to believe. Bertrand Russell or John Dewey might solve a philosophical problem, but how could I? After all, I was taking my first graduate course, and had mastered few of the classics. How could I solve a philosophical problem? Furthermore, who would be interested in reading my views?

The professor told us that the first article we were to discuss had not yet appeared in print. This announcement added to my growing wonder, because I had never read a professional article prior to its publication. He proceeded to distribute the mimeographed pages of this unpublished manuscript by a scholar unknown to me. Our job, we were told, was to analyze this essay, to decide whether its main contention was correct.

Our professor then approached the blackboard and wrote down several statements. He turned round and asked us whether the last statement followed from the previous ones.

A student raised his hand and launched into a long speech full of technical terms and references to the works of a variety of medieval thinkers. The professor listened intently, his face first expressing hope, then turning to disappointment. "I'm afraid I don't understand much of what you said," he replied. "I didn't ask anything about any medieval philosophers. I only asked if the last statement is implied by the preceding ones. What do you think about that?" The student shrugged his shoulders and looked frustrated.

Another student confidently raised her hand and inquired whether the issue had not been handled adequately in an article that had appeared several years before in a leading philosophical journal. The professor responded, "I really don't know. I haven't read that article. But perhaps you could tell us: Is the last statement I have written on the blackboard implied by the preceding ones?" The student replied that she couldn't remember. "But," the professor continued, "there's nothing to remember. The statements are on the board. Does the last follow from the others, or doesn't it?" She offered no response.

Never in my study of philosophy had I witnessed such an approach. I was unfamiliar with the medieval thinkers to whom the first student had referred, and I knew nothing of the article to which the second student had alluded. The answer to the professor's question, however, was not to be found in a dusty tome or dog-eared journal. We were being asked to think, to philosophize.

Suddenly I understood what the professor meant when he had said that we ourselves would try to solve philosophical problems, and at that moment I experienced a remarkable sense of intellectual liberation. I raised my hand and presented my opinion, something I had been reluctant to do in other classes, for fear that my ignorance of philosophical literature would be apparent to all. The professor indicated that my comment was interesting, but he inquired how I would deal with a certain objection. I was unsure how to respond and sat silently, pondering the matter. By the time an idea came to me, the class was over.

I immediately decided to visit him and pursue my point. Other professors were usually available for conferences with students only three or four hours a week. This professor met with his students three or four afternoons a week—all afternoon. I was accustomed to waiting on line an hour or more to see a popular teacher. This professor had placed a sheet on his office door, so that students could sign up in advance for fifteen- or thirty-minute appointments.

I ventured in one afternoon and began presenting my ideas. Soon he interrupted, "Write a paper for me." I had not intended to write my views down, believing that I needed only to communicate them orally. He made clear that he believed putting one's ideas in written form was indispensable to precise thinking.

I went home, worked harder than I could ever remember, and the following week brought him a paper. He told me he would read it and get back to me. Several days later, eager to learn his reaction, I knocked at his door before the announced office hours and timidly inquired whether he had yet read my essay. He replied that he was busy writing and could not speak with me but would return the paper. He passed it through the half-open door and said he would see me later. On the front page was his comment, the substance of which was that after further work the paper ought to be published and should serve as a section of my dissertation.

I was stunned. Here I was in my first month of graduate study, and I was being told I had written something worth publishing and had already, in essence, completed part of my dissertation.

For the next two years I devoted myself to justifying his confidence. I attended every class he taught and wrote paper after paper. I signed up for conferences several times a week and often waited near his office to take advantage of free time created by the cancellation of a scheduled appointment. He never begrudged me a moment but continued to urge me to write more and to come in to discuss what I had written. The hours we spent together became the focus of my life.

I no longer doubted my choice of career, and, through his patience and efforts, I became a philosopher. Incidentally, his reaction to that first paper proved prophetic, because three years after writing it, I received my Ph.D., and my dissertation included the already published material from that initial effort.[3]

In sum, while certain graduate faculty members neglect, mistreat, or even ruin those they are supposed to guide, other faculty members sustain students and help them strive to reach their goals. Thus does graduate education epitomize the basest abuses and the highest ideals of ethics in academia.

APPENDIX A

∼

Searching for Administrators
The Missing Step

Every year numerous colleges and universities conduct elaborate searches for academic administrators, including all manner of deans, vice presidents, and provosts. In each case, the steps are remarkably similar: A search committee is formed, an advertisement is placed, a hundred or so applications are received, the list is shortened, letters of reference are obtained, another cut is made, campus interviews are conducted, recommendations are presented, and the final decision is announced.

The process is invariably exhausting, but the results are often disappointing. The candidate who appeared confident and genial during interviews may turn out in office to be ineffective, evasive, or irresponsible. The rejected candidate whose crusty manner or candid opinions put off some committee members may be offered an administrative position elsewhere and become widely admired for trustworthiness, conscientiousness, and acumen.

Some mistakes are, of course, inevitable. But at least judgments should be made on the basis of the best available evidence. At present, however, committees frequently deliberate in the dark. They proceed as if the most important information were to be found in a curriculum vitae, letters from a candidate's supporters, and observations of a candidate's demeanor in a series of brief meetings.

The most reliable indicator of future performance, however, is past performance. And the quality of past performance is not found in a vita, a supporter's letter, or a brief question-and-answer session. The vita lists the positions held, not the quality of performance in each position. An interview tells more about the candidate's surface personality and oral facility than sagacity or dependability. As for letters of recommendation, they are notoriously unhelpful. Even Stalin could have obtained glowing letters from three of his colleagues, testifying to his consultative management style and creative leadership.

The best evidence is to be found not in what a candidate's friends say but in the judgments attested to by a variety of individuals who hold responsible positions at the candidate's campus. What does the chair of the senate say about the candidate's commitment to upholding the appropriate authority of the faculty? What does the chair of the curriculum committee report about the candidate's attitude toward rethinking requirements? What does the chair of the appointments committee tell about the candidate's standards for appointments, promotions, and tenure? What do department chairs relate about the candidate's approach to making budgetary decisions? Do the chairs find the candidate accessible, resourceful, fair-minded, and committed to enhancing academic quality? Do other administrators or administrative assistants view the candidate as thoughtful or impulsive, patient or irritable, collegial or overbearing, forgiving or vindictive?

During an interview of a few hours, the candidate may maintain a false front to members of a search committee. But those who have long observed the candidate's character, including at times of personal confrontation or moments of institutional crisis, are beyond being fooled.

Thus when the list of finalists is determined, each should be informed that at least one or, better yet, several members of the committee will be speaking to or, preferably, visiting with key members of the academic community at the candidate's school. While a candidate may request that a particular person not be contacted if that individual is thought to be negatively biased, a candidate who objects to the whole procedure should be passed over. For however strong the candidate's desire to retain confidentiality, it is outweighed by the committee's obligation to make the soundest possible decision.

If the information thus obtained suggests that the administrator's performance was less than first-rate, the committee may reasonably assume the person will do no better at the next position. The administrator who micromanaged at one campus is a good bet to try to do so at the next. The administrator who wasted money at one institution is unlikely to spend it wisely at another. During interviews, a candidate may give the impression of welcoming constructive criticism, but if numerous colleagues who have worked with the person report to the contrary, their testimony should be considered decisive.

Indeed, were I required to select an administrator by relying either on a vita, letters of recommendation, and interviews, or solely on the judgments of numerous previous colleagues, I would choose the latter. Search committees, however, do not face this forced option. They can continue to consider the usual information while supplementing it with the best available evidence. Such a procedure would lead to greater satisfaction with the performance of those we entrust with administrative responsibilities. In the end, achieving that goal is the measure of success for every search committee.[1]

APPENDIX B

~

Two Concepts of Affirmative Action

In March 1961, less than two months after assuming office, President John F. Kennedy issued Executive Order 10925, establishing the President's Committee on Equal Employment Opportunity. Its mission was to end discrimination in employment by the government and its contractors. The order required every federal contract to include the pledge that "The contractor will not discriminate against any employe[e] or applicant for employment because of race, creed, color, or national origin. The contractor will take affirmative action to ensure that applicants are employed, and that employe[e]s are treated during employment, without regard to their race, creed, color, or national origin."

Here, for the first time in the context of civil rights, the government called for "affirmative action." The term meant taking appropriate steps to eradicate the then widespread practices of racial, religious, and ethnic discrimination.[1] The goal, as the Pesident stated, was "equal opportunity in employment." In other words, *procedural* affirmative action, as I shall call it, was instituted to ensure that applicants for positions would be judged without any consideration of their race, religion, or national origin. These criteria were declared irrelevant. Taking them into account was forbidden.

The Civil Rights Act of 1964 restated and broadened the application of this principle. Title VI declared that "No person in the United States shall, on the ground of race, color or national origin, be excluded from participation in, be denied the benefits of, or be subjected to discrimination under any program or activity receiving Federal financial assistance."

Before one year had passed, however, President Lyndon B. Johnson argued that fairness required more than a commitment to such procedural affirmative action. In his 1965 commencement address at Howard University, he said, "You do not take a person who for years has been hobbled by chains and liberate him, bring him up to the starting line of a race and then say, 'you're free to compete with all the others,' and still justly believe that you have been completely fair."

Several months later, President Johnson issued Executive Order 11246, stating that "It is the policy of the Government of the United States to provide equal opportunity in Federal employment for all qualified persons, to prohibit discrimination in employment because of race, creed, color or national origin, and to promote the full realization of equal employment opportunity through a positive, continuing program in each department and agency." Two years later the order was amended to prohibit discrimination on the basis of sex.

While the aim of President Johnson's order is stated in language similar to that of President Kennedy's, President Johnson's abolished the Committee on Equal Employment Opportunity, transferred its responsibilities to the Secretary of Labor, and authorized the Secretary to "adopt such rules and regulations and issue such orders as he deems necessary and appropriate to achieve the purposes thereof."

Acting on this mandate, the Department of Labor in December 1971, during the administration of President Richard M. Nixon, issued Revised Order No. 4, requiring all federal contractors to develop "an acceptable affirmative action program," including "an analysis of areas within which the contractor is deficient in the utilization of minority groups and women, and further, goals and timetables to which the contractor's good faith efforts must be directed to correct the deficiencies." Contractors were instructed to take the term "minority groups" to refer to "Negroes, American Indians, Orientals, and Spanish Surnamed Americans." (No guidance was given as to whether having only one parent, grandparent, or great-grandparent from a group would suffice to establish group membership.) The concept of "underutilization," according to the Revised Order, meant "having fewer minorities or women in a particular job classification than would reasonably be expected by their availability." "Goals" were not to be "rigid and inflexible quotas," but "targets reasonably attainable by means of applying every good faith effort to make all aspects of the entire affirmative action program work."[2]

Such preferential affirmative action, as I shall call it, requires that attention be paid to the same criteria of race, sex, and ethnicity that procedural affirmative action deems irrelevant. Is such use of these criteria justifiable in employment decisions?[3]

Return to President Johnson's claim that a person hobbled by discrimination cannot in fairness be expected to be competitive. How are we to determine which specific individuals are entitled to a compensatory advantage? To decide each case on its own merits would be possible, but this approach would undermine the argument for instituting preferential affirmative action on a group basis. For if some members of a group are able to compete, why not others? Thus defenders of preferential affirmative action maintain that the group, not the individual, is to be judged. If the group has suffered discrimination, then all its members are to be treated as hobbled runners.

Note, however, that while a hobbled runner, provided with a sufficient lead in a race, may cross the finish line first, giving that person an edge prevents the individual from being considered as fast a runner as others. An equally fast runner does not need an advantage to be competitive. This entire racing analogy thus encourages stereotypical thinking. For example, recall those men who played in baseball's Negro Leagues. That these athletes were barred from competing in the Major Leagues is the greatest stain on the history of the sport. While they suffered discrimination, these players were as proficient as their counterparts in the Major Leagues. They needed only to be judged by the same criteria as all others, and ensuring such equality of consideration is the essence of procedural affirmative action.

Granted, if individuals are unprepared or ill-equipped to compete, then they ought to be helped to try to achieve their goals. But such aid is appropriate for all who need it, not merely for members of particular racial, sexual, or ethnic groups.

Victims of discrimination deserve compensation. Former players in the Negro Leagues ought to receive special consideration in the arrangement of pension plans and any other benefits formerly denied these athletes due to unfair treatment. The case for such compensation, however, does not imply that present Black players vying for jobs in the Major Leagues should be evaluated in any other way than their performance on the field. To assume their inability to compete is derogatory and erroneous.

Such considerations have led recent defenders of preferential affirmative action to rely less heavily on any argument that implies the attribution of noncompetitiveness to an entire population.[4] Instead, the emphasis has been placed on recognizing the benefits society is said to derive from encouraging expression of the varied experiences, outlooks, and values of members of different groups.

This approach makes a virtue of what has come to be called "diversity."[5] As a defense of preferential affirmative action, diversity has at least two advantages. First, those previously excluded are now included not as a favor to them but as a means of enriching all. Second, no one is viewed as hobbled; each competes on a par, although with varied strengths.

Note that diversity requires preferential hiring. Those who enhance diversity are to be preferred to those who do not. Those preferred, however, are not being chosen because of their deficiency; the larger group is deficient, lacking diversity.

What does it mean to say that a group lacks diversity? Or to put the question another way, could we decide, for example, which member of a ten-person group to eliminate in order to decrease most markedly its diversity?

So stated, the question is reminiscent of a provocative puzzle in *The Tyranny of Testing*, a 1962 book by the scientist Banesh Hoffman. In this attack on the importance placed on multiple-choice tests, he quotes the following letter to the editor of the *Times* of London:

> Sir—Among the "odd one out" type of questions which my son had to answer for a school entrance examination was: "Which is the odd one out among cricket, football, billiards, and hockey?" [In England "football" refers to the game Americans call "soccer," and "hockey" here refers to "field hockey."] The letter continued: I said billiards because it is the only one played indoors. A colleague says football because it is the

only one in which the ball is not struck by an implement. A neighbour says cricket because in all the other games the object is to put the ball into a net. . . . Could any of your readers put me out of my misery by stating what is the correct answer?

A day later the *Times* printed the following two letters:

> Sir.—"Billiards" is the obvious answer . . . because it is the only one of the games listed which is not a team game.
>
> Sir.—. . . football is the odd one out because . . . it is played with an inflated ball as compared with the solid ball used in each of the other three.

Hoffman then continued his own discussion:

> When I had read these three letters it seemed to me that good cases had been made for football and billiards, and that the case for cricket was particularly clever. . . . At first I thought this made hockey easily the worst of the four choices and, in effect, ruled it out. But then I realized that the very fact that hockey was the only one that could be thus ruled out gave it so striking a quality of separateness as to make it an excellent answer after all—perhaps the best. Fortunately, for my peace of mind, it soon occurred to me that hockey is the only one of the four games that is played with a curved implement.

The following day the *Times* published yet another letter, this from a philosophically sophisticated thinker.

> Sir.—[The author of the original letter] . . . has put his finger on what has long been a matter of great amusement to me. Of the four—cricket, football, billiards, hockey—each is unique in a multitude of respects. For example, billiards is the only one played with more than one ball at once, the only one played on a green cloth and not on a field. . . . It seems to me that those who have been responsible for inventing this kind of brain teaser have been ignorant of the elementary philosophical fact that every thing is at once unique and a member of a wider class.

With this sound principle in mind, return to the problem of deciding which member of a ten-person group to eliminate in order to decrease most markedly its diversity. Unless the sort of diversity is specified, the question has no rational answer.

In searches for college and university faculty members, we know what sorts of diversity are typically of present concern: race, sex, and certain ethnicities. Why should these characteristics be given special regard?

Consider, for example, other nonacademic respects in which prospective faculty appointees can differ: age, religion, nationality, regional background, economic class, social stratum, military experience, bodily appearance, physical soundness, sexual orientation, marital status, ethical standards, political commitments, and cultural values. Why should we not seek diversity of these sorts?

To some extent schools do. Many colleges and universities indicate in advertisements for faculty positions that the schools seek veterans or persons with disabilities. The City University of New York requires all searches to give preference to individuals of Italian-American descent.

The crucial point is that the appeal to diversity never favors any particular candidate. Each one adds to some sort of diversity but not another. In a department of ten, one individual might be the only Black, another the only woman, another the only bachelor, another the only veteran, another the only one over fifty, another the only Catholic, another the only Republican, another the only Scandinavian, another the only socialist, and the tenth the only Southerner.

Suppose the suggestion is made that the sorts of diversity to be sought are those of groups that have suffered discrimination. This approach leads to another problem, clearly put by John Kekes:

> It is true that American blacks, Native Americans, Hispanics, and women have suffered injustice as a group. But so have homosexuals, epileptics, the urban and the rural poor, the physically ugly, those whose careers were ruined by McCarthyism, prostitutes, the obese, and so forth.
>
> There have been some attempts to deny that there is an analogy between these two classes of victims. It has been said that the first were unjustly discriminated against due to racial or sexual prejudice and that this is not true of the second. This is indeed so. But why should we accept the suggestion . . . that the only form of injustice relevant to preferential treatment is that which is due to racial or sexual prejudice?

Injustice occurs in many forms, and those who value justice will surely object to all of them.[6]

Kekes's reasoning is cogent. In addition, another difficulty looms for the proposal to seek diversity only of groups that have suffered discrimination. For diversity is supposed to be valued not as compensation to the disadvantaged but as a means of enriching all.

Consider, for example, a department in which most of the faculty members are women. In certain fields such as nursing and elementary education, such departments are common. If diversity by sex is of value, then such a department, when making its next appointment, should prefer a man. Yet men as a group have not been victims of discrimination. To achieve valued sorts of diversity, the question is not which groups have been discriminated against, but which valued groups are not represented. The question thus reappears as to which sorts of diversity are to be most highly valued. I know of no compelling answer.

Seeking to justify preferential affirmative action in terms of its contribution to diversity raises another difficulty. For preferential affirmative action is commonly defended as a temporary rather than a permanent measure.[7] Preferential affirmative action to achieve diversity, however, is not temporary.

Suppose it were. Then once an institution had appointed an appropriate number of members of a particular group, preferential affirmative action would no longer be in effect. Yet the institution may later find that it has too few members of that group. Because lack of valuable diversity is presumably no more acceptable at one time than another, preferential affirmative action would have to be reinstituted. Thereby it would in effect become a permanent policy.

Why do so many of its defenders wish it to be only transitional? They believe the policy was instituted in response to irrelevant criteria for appointment having been mistakenly treated as relevant. To adopt any policy that continues to treat essentially irrelevant criteria as relevant is to share the guilt of those who discriminated originally. Irrelevant criteria should be recognized as such and abandoned as soon as feasible.

Some defenders of preferential affirmative action argue, however, that an individuals' race, sex, or ethnicity is germane to fulfilling the responsibilities of a faculty member. They believe, therefore, that preferential affirmative action should be a permanent feature of search processes, because it takes account of criteria that should be considered in every appointment.

At least three reasons have been offered to justify the claim that those of a particular race, sex, or ethnicity are well-suited to be faculty members: first, they would be especially effective teachers of any student who shares their race, sex, or ethnicity;[8] second, they would be particularly insightful researchers because of their experiencing the world from distinctive standpoints;[9] third, they would be role models, demonstrating that those of a particular race, sex, or ethnicity can be effective faculty members.[10]

Consider each of these claims in turn. As to the presumed teaching effectiveness of the individuals in question, no empirical study supports the claim.[11] But assume compelling evidence were presented. It would have no implications for individual cases. A particular person who does not share race, sex, or ethnicity with students might teach them superbly. An individual of the students' own race, sex, or ethnicity might be ineffective. Regardless of statistical correlations, what is crucial is that individuals be able to teach effectively all sorts of students, and seeking individuals who give evidence of satisfying this criterion is entirely consistent with procedural affirmative action. But knowing an individual's race, sex, or ethnicity does not reveal whether that person will be effective in the classroom.

Do members of a particular race, sex, or ethnicity share a distinctive intellectual perspective that enhances their scholarship? Celia Wolf-Devine has aptly described this claim as a form of "stereotyping" that is "demeaning." As she puts it, "A Hispanic who is a Republican is no less a Hispanic, and a woman who is not a feminist is no less a woman."[12] Furthermore, are Hispanic men and women supposed to have the same point of view in virtue of their common ethnicity, or are they supposed to have different points of view in virtue of their different genders?

If our standpoints are thought to be determined by our race, sex, and ethnicity, why not also by the numerous other significant respects in which people differ, such as age, religion, sexual orientation, and so on? Because each of us is unique, can anyone else share my point of view?

That my own experience is my own is a tautology that does not imply the keenness of my insight into my experience. The victim of a crime may as a result embrace an outlandish theory of racism. But neither who you are nor what you experience guarantees the truth of your theories.

To be an effective researcher calls for discernment, imagination, and perseverance. These attributes are not tied to one's race, sex, ethnicity, age, or religion. Black scholars, for example, may be more inclined to study Black literature than are non-Black scholars. But some non-Black literary critics are more interested in and more knowledgeable about Black literature than are some Black literary critics. Why make decisions based on fallible racial generalizations when judgments of individual merit are obtainable and more reliable?

Perhaps the answer lies in the claim that only those of a particular race, sex, or ethnicity can serve as role models, exemplifying to members of a particular group the possibility of their success. Again, no empirical study supports the claim, but it has often been taken as self-evident that, for instance, only a woman can be a role model for a woman, only a Black for a Black, and only a Catholic for a Catholic. In other words, the crucial feature of a person is supposed to be not what the person does but who the person is.

The logic of the situation, however, is not so clear. Consider, for example, a Black man who is a Catholic. Presumably he serves as a role model for Blacks, men, and Catholics. Does he serve as a role model for Black women, or can only a Black woman serve that purpose? Does he serve as a role model for all Catholics or only for those who are Black? Can I serve as a role model for anyone else, because no one else shares all my characteristics? Perhaps I can serve as a role model for everyone else, because everyone else belongs to at least one group to which I belong.

Putting aside these conundrums, the critical point is supposed to be that in a field in which discrimination has been rife, a successful individual who belongs to the discriminated group demonstrates that members of the group can succeed in that field. Obviously success is possible without a role model, for the first successful individual had none. But suppose persuasive evidence were offered that a role model, while not necessary, sometimes is helpful, not only to those who belong to the group in question but also to those prone to believe that no members of the group can perform effectively within the field. Role models would then both encourage members of a group that had suffered discrimination and discourage further discrimination against the group.

To serve these purposes, however, the person chosen would need to be viewed as having been selected by the same criteria as all others. If not, members of the group that has suffered discrimination as well as those prone to discriminate would be confirmed in their common view that members of the group never would have been chosen unless membership in the group had been taken into account. Those who suffered discrimination would conclude that it still exists, while those prone to discriminate would conclude that members of the group lack the necessary attributes to compete equally.

How can we ensure that a person chosen for a position has been selected by the same criteria as all others? Preferential affirmative action fails to serve the purpose, because by definition it differentiates among people on the basis of criteria other than performance. The approach that ensures merit selection is procedural affirmative action. It maximizes equal opportunity by demanding vigilance against every form of discrimination.

The policy of appointing others than the best qualified has not produced a harmonious society in which prejudice is transcended and all enjoy the benefits of self-esteem. Rather, the practice has bred doubts about the abilities of those chosen while generating resentment in those passed over.

Procedural affirmative action had barely begun before it was replaced by preferential affirmative action. The difficulties with the latter are now clear. Before deeming them necessary evils in the struggle to overcome pervasive prejudice, why not try scrupulous enforcement of procedural affirmative action? We might thereby most directly achieve that equitable society so ardently desired by every person of good will.[13]

APPENDIX C

~

Why Not Tell the Truth?

A fundamental principle of academic ethics is that the announcement of any available faculty or administrative position should make clear whatever special criteria the institution has established for choosing among applicants. Criteria not specified should not be used.

Today virtually every college or university advertising a position in *The Chronicle of Higher Education* describes itself as an "Equal Opportunity/Affirmative Action Employer," sometimes adding that it "welcomes and encourages applications from women and minority candidates" (and occasionally "veterans" or "persons with disabilities"). While such phrases are always supposed to signify that the college or university does not engage in discrimination, sometimes the same words are also intended to convey the important message that the institution strongly prefers or will only give serious consideration to members of specific groups.

In fairness to all applicants, shouldn't departments and schools be explicit about such matters? If agreement has been reached internally that membership in particular groups is to be given strong weight in the decision procedure, shouldn't the announcement of the position say so? And in instances in which an institution has decided to fill a position only if a qualified member of a particular group or groups can be found, shouldn't this information, too, be stated candidly?

Several university presidents recently announced that they had committed their institutions to appointing, within a fixed time, a specific number of faculty members from certain groups. At one university the administration's policy is to make available a faculty position for any department that finds a qualified Black candidate. At another university the Board of Trustees has created five new faculty positions designated specifically for Black scholars. Search committees at those institutions are instructed to make choices that will help achieve the stated objectives. Shouldn't announcements of positions at those schools inform potential applicants of the special situations, so that people who are, and people who are not, members of the groups in question can decide whether to apply in light of full information about the conditions governing the searches?

Not everyone agrees about the most effective and equitable actions colleges can take to remedy injustice. But whatever the criteria in effect for an appointment, the faculty members and administrators who established them surely considered them to be within ethical and legal bounds.

Why not state these criteria publicly, without ambiguity or deception? Why not tell the truth?[1]

APPENDIX D

~

Taking Teaching Seriously

College and university administrators frequently claim to care deeply about the quality of teaching at their institutions. But too often their actions belie their words.

For instance, which candidate for a faculty position is usually viewed as more attractive, the promising researcher or the promising teacher? Who usually receives the larger salary increase, the successful researcher or the successful teacher? When a faculty member receives an offer from another institution, is more effort usually made to retain an outstanding researcher or an outstanding teacher? Who usually receives such offers, the famed researcher or the famed teacher? Granted, the scholar-teacher is the ideal, but who is more likely to receive tenure: a top-notch researcher who is dull in the classroom, or a top-notch teacher whose scholarship is thin?

If presidents, provosts, and deans were as concerned about teaching as they say, their commitment would be demonstrated by policies quite different from those typically now in place.

First, during a campus interview a candidate for a faculty position would be expected to give not only a research paper but also a talk on an elementary topic, organized and presented as if for introductory students. Only those candidates whose teaching performance was proficient would be taken seriously for an appointment.

Second, when salary raises were distributed, excellence in teaching would be weighed just as heavily as excellence in research. Giving teaching prizes to a select few while rewarding research for the many would be no more common than giving research prizes to a select few while rewarding teaching for the many.

Third, just as research is evaluated by peer review, so teaching would be. Popularity among students is a positive sign for a teacher, just as having a book on the best-seller list is a positive sign for a researcher, but neither accomplishment ensures academic quality. We care enough about research to undertake an elaborate review of a professor's scholarship; we ought to care enough about teaching to undertake an equally elaborate review of a professor's work in the classroom. Such a review should involve input from departmental colleagues who would visit the professor's classes and examine syllabi, examinations, and test papers to assess teaching performance. The more an institution is concerned about teaching, the more effort will be made in evaluating it.

Fourth, a corollary of serious evaluation of teaching is the willingness to differentiate among levels of effectiveness. We recognize the differences between research that is incompetent, or barely competent, or mediocre, or strong, or superb; the same distinctions apply to teaching. Not every sound researcher is a serious candidate for a Nobel Prize or its equivalent; neither is every sound teacher a serious candidate for the teaching Hall of Fame. Describing all teachers simply as "good" or "not so good" is a sign that teaching is not taken seriously. An individual may be said to be a good teacher; the key question is: how good?

Fifth, an outstanding researcher may be awarded tenure even with a weak performance in the classroom. An analogous policy should be in effect for an outstanding teacher with a weak performance in research. Again, the ideal candidate excels as researcher and teacher, but if an occasional exception is made so as not to lose a researcher of national stature, so an occasional exception should also be made so as not to lose an extraordinary teacher.

Sixth, an institution sometimes seeks to recruit an outstanding researcher to enable a department to enhance its national reputation. But has any school ever recruited an outstanding teacher to enable a department to strengthen its offerings to students? I don't recall ever seeing an advertisement seeking such an individual, but a school committed to teaching would from time to time conduct such searches.

Seventh, if graduate schools cared about teaching, they would require courses in methods of instruction for all students who are to be recommended for faculty appointments. Such courses should involve future professors in discussing and practicing all phases of the teaching process, including motivating students, organizing materials, clarifying concepts, guiding discussions, constructing examinations, and grading papers. Emphasis should also be placed on the crucial importance and multifaceted nature of a teacher's ethical obligations.

Eighth, letters of recommendation would provide details not only about a candidate's research but also about the candidate's teaching. At present, such letters usually contain a perfunctory sentence or two, assuring the reader that although the writer has never actually seen the candidate teach, given the candidate's intelligence and winning personality, the writer is sure that the candidate will be effective in the classroom. After reading hundreds of such letters, I wonder where all the ineffective teachers come from.

Ninth, just as faculty members are given release time to pursue their research, so they would be given such time to develop new courses, syllabi, and methodologies. They would also be offered the opportunity to attend a center for teaching effectiveness, working with the guidance of master teachers to strengthen pedagogic skills.

Tenth and finally, at a school seriously concerned with teaching, classrooms would be open to all qualified persons, including any interested members of the faculty who wished to sit in. Physicians hone their own skills by watching colleagues conduct medical procedures; similarly, teachers can learn by observation. Furthermore, teachers who may be visited by peers are apt to devote greater attention to presentations. Open classrooms thus benefit all.

At schools where these policies are in effect, teaching will not be overshadowed by research. Instead, teaching will be taken seriously. And at such institutions those who pay the tuition bills can depend on receiving the quality of instruction to which they are entitled.[1]

APPENDIX E

~

Teaching Graduate Students to Teach

Several years ago I offered our doctoral students a fourteen-week, credit-bearing course titled "Teaching Philosophy." The goal was to prepare new or inexperienced teachers to meet the challenges of offering effective instruction to undergraduates. The results were dramatic.

While some class time was spent discussing ethical obligations and pedagogical principles, as well as preparing sample syllabi and examinations, most of the hours were devoted to practice. Each of the seventeen students gave a series of short presentations to their classmates: a five-minute account of a nonphilosophical topic of their choice, a ten-minute introduction to a philosophical subject, another ten-minute development of that subject, and a final somewhat longer talk on a different philosophical issue. After each presentation, the speaker received immediate, detailed feedback from me and the other students.

At first, most of the participants were extremely nervous as they stood before the audience. They mumbled, talked too fast, laughed self-consciously, and stared at the ceiling, the blackboard, or their notes, avoiding eye contact with those they were supposed to be addressing. They made little attempt to interest their listeners in the subject. They presumed knowledge the audience didn't possess. They used technical terms without explaining them. They became lost in minutiae. In short, these beginners displayed all the pedagogical shortcomings that turn too many college classrooms into scenes of boredom and confusion.

But whereas most instructors who communicate inadequately are never called to account, in this case weak presentations brought forth a series of constructive suggestions for improvement. Not only did these help the speaker, but they reinforced for all students the elements of sound instruction and the precautions needed to avoid pedagogic pitfalls.

Soon noticeable improvements occurred. The students began to speak more slowly and clearly, they offered motivation and perspective to their audience, and they organized their talks so that ideas were presented in a comprehensible sequence. Most remarkably, some students whose initial stage fright had made them seem somber or remote turned out, after becoming more at ease, to be engaging and even humorous.

Students whose presentations showed marked improvement received generous plaudits from the others in the class, and the developing esprit de corps encouraged all to try to enhance their performance. Before long, most of the talks were quite compelling, and the few students who continued to struggle at least were conscious of the reasons for their lack of success.

After listening to each of the seventeen final presentations, instead of oral reactions being offered, all the students wrote evaluations and suggestions that I later shared on an anonymous basis at a personal conference with each member of the class. Perhaps I can convey most effectively what we accomplished by quoting a sampling of the comments, each containing a condensed version of one student's exact words.

- Energetic, attention-grabbing, and polished presentation. Nice motivation, leading expertly to the topic to be discussed. Smooth interaction with students; handled comments well without distraction. Clear exposition of the issues at hand. Should avoid using notes too much. Rehearse so there is no need to refresh during the presentation. Should slow down a bit.
- Way too many "OKs." Too much looking at the board. No attempt at motivation. Nice pace. Many opportunities for dis-

cussion passed over. Though he asked us to raise our hands if we had a comment, there didn't seem to be any opportunities to do so.

- Powerful example used to motivate interest, but the wind-up went on too long. Clear, obviously well-prepared. The pace at times was a bit fast, perhaps because of nervousness. You asked questions but mostly answered them yourself. Along with the longish set-up, I think this made for a certain disengagement on the part of the class. It's hard to hold interest by just talking to the class. You need to connect to them.

- Don't get defensive in response to a difficult student answer, but use the answer as best you can to get back on track. Became much more comfortable toward the end, warmed up, relaxed. You became able to use emphasis and tone to create drama, suspense, and interest. Nice, personable manner, and slow, clear pace.

- Don't look at the board like you're expecting it to do something. Make sure you're making eye contact with us. Your tone is calm and reassuring. Great use of example and class participation to build the point. You use the class and their answers well. It becomes a fun discussion.

- The pacing was a little fast in some places. Examples worked well, but I think that discussing them further, especially by asking students to participate at some point, would have worked even better. Overall, a lively and interesting presentation of a difficult topic.

- There's no motivation, no gateway into the issue. Way too attached to notes. Put them down. We desperately need examples. There's too much terminology tossed about, and nothing relevant or playful to tie it down. The main thrust of your attention is the board. Make the students your primary focus.

- Considerably more comfortable and casual than in previous presentations. Good use of humor to engage audience. Much better job of making eye contact and connecting with the class. A lot of information is covered a little too quickly. It would be a good idea to use the board to set up an outline and keep track of key terms. But overall so much better. Congratulations!

I doubt that any course can turn poor teachers into great ones. But if taken during those formative years of graduate study when individuals are most likely to welcome help, the advice provided can turn inaudible, unclear, or disorganized speakers into audible, clear, and organized ones. Most important, it can turn thoughtless instructors into thoughtful ones, the critical step on the path toward more effective and responsible teaching.[1]

~

Notes

Preface

1. To protect the identities of individuals referred to in this book, names have been omitted, and indications of gender have been masked.

2. Regarding the selection of academic administrators, see appendix A.

Chapter One

1. Professor X, *This Beats Working for a Living: The Dark Secrets of a College Professor* (New Rochelle, N.Y.: Arlington House, 1973), 11.

2. John Stuart Mill, *On Liberty* (New York: Liberal Arts Press, 1956), 25.

3. Mill, *On Liberty*, 21.

Chapter Two

1. Alfred North Whitehead, *The Aims of Education and Other Essays* (New York: Free Press, 1967 [1929]), 36.

2. Whitehead, *The Aims of Education*, 34.

3. Gilbert Highet, *The Art of Teaching* (New York: Random House, 1954 [1950]), 132.

4. Those who believe in the importance of recognizing formally a student's level of effort or improvement should favor awarding supplementary grades for these special purposes rather than distorting the recognized meaning of grades, thereby undermining their ordinary uses.

5. Charles A. Reich, *The Greening of America* (New York: Random House, 1970), 226–27.

6. Steven M. Cahn, *The Eclipse of Excellence* (Washington, D.C.: Public Affairs Press, 1973).

7. O. B. Hardison Jr., *Toward Freedom and Dignity: The Humanities and the Idea of Humanity* (Baltimore: Johns Hopkins Press, 1972), 139.

8. Hardison, *Toward Freedom and Dignity*, 140.

9. Hardison, *Toward Freedom and Dignity*, 147.

10. Sidney Hook, *Education for Modern Man: A New Perspective* (New York: Alfred A. Knopf, 1963), 203, 207.

11. Donald H. Naftulin, John E. Ware Jr., and Frank A. Donnelly, "The Doctor Fox Lecture: A Paradigm of Educational Seduction," *Journal of Medical Education* 48 (1973): 630–35.

12. M. C. Wittrock and Arthur A. Lumsdaine, "Instructional Psychology," *Annual Review of Psychology* 28 (1977): 417–59.

13. Charles Frankel, *Education and the Barricades* (New York: Norton, 1968), 30–31.

14. Ross Vasta and Robert F. Sarmiento, "Liberal Grading Improves Evaluations but Not Performance," *Journal of Educational Psychology* 71 (1979): 207–11.

15. Charles B. Schultz, "Some Limits to the Validity and Usefulness of Student Rating of Teachers: An Argument for Caution," *Educational Research Quarterly* 3 (1978): 12–27.

Chapter Three

1. *Ethics of the Fathers*, trans. Hyman Goldin (New York: Hebrew Publishing Company, 1962), 2:21.

2. Sidney Hook, *Education for Modern Man*, 155.

3. Eva T. H. Brann, *Paradoxes of Education in a Republic* (Chicago: University of Chicago Press, 1979), 62.

4. Brann, *Paradoxes of Education*, 3, 74.

5. John Dewey, *Democracy and Education: The Middle Works of John Dewey, 1899–1924*, ed. Jo Ann Boydston (Carbondale: Southern Illinois University Press, 1980), 9:248, 250.

6. John Herman Randall Jr., *Aristotle* (New York: Columbia University Press, 1960), 1–2.

7. Randall, *Aristotle*, 1.

Chapter Four

1. I here pass over the thicket of moral and legal issues related to affirmative action, for they transcend academic ethics. Differing judgments about appropriate university policies in this area are found in Steven M. Cahn, ed., *Affirmative Action and the University: A Philosophical Inquiry* (Philadelphia: Temple University Press, 1993). A balanced presentation of more general issues at the heart of the controversy is Steven M. Cahn, ed., *The Affirmative Action Debate*, 2nd ed. (New York: Routledge, 2002). My own views on the controversial subject of affirmative action in faculty appointments are offered in appendix B.

2. Regarding truth in advertising for academic positions, see appendix C.

3. Sidney Hook, *Education and the Taming of Power* (La Salle, Ill.: Open Court, 1973), 213.

4. Administrators often claim that they are deeply concerned about quality of teaching, but their actions frequently tell otherwise. Regarding this situation, see appendix D.

5. "Academic Freedom and Tenure: 1940 Statement on Principles and Interpretive Comments," in *AAUP: Policy Documents and Reports* (Washington, D.C.: American Association of University Professors, 1984), 4.

6. "1982 Recommended Institutional Regulations on Academic Freedom and Tenure," in *AAUP: Policy Documents and Reports* (Washington, D.C.: American Association of University Professors, 1984), 26–27.

Chapter Five

1. Jaroslav Pelikan, *Scholarship and Its Survival* (Princeton, N.J.: Carnegie Foundation for the Advancement of Teaching, 1983), 26.

2. My experience teaching such a course is described in appendix E.

3. The professor was Richard Taylor.

Appendix A

1. This essay originally appeared in the *AAHE Bulletin* 50, no. 2 (1997). Reprinted with permission of the American Association of Higher Education and Assessment.

Appendix B

1. A comprehensive history of one well-documented case of such discrimination is Dan A. Oren, *Joining the Club: A History of Jews and Yale* (New Haven, Conn.: Yale University Press, 1985). Prior to the end of World War II, no Jew had ever been appointed to the rank of full professor in Yale College.

2. 41 C.F.R. 60-2.12. The Order provides no indication of whether a "good faith effort" implies only showing preference among equally qualified candidates (the "tie-breaking" model), preferring a strong candidate to an even stronger one (the "plus factor" model), preferring a merely qualified candidate to a strongly qualified one (the "trumping" model), or canceling a search unless a qualified candidate of the preferred sort is available (the "quota" model). A significant source of misunderstanding about affirmative action results from both the government's failure to clarify which type of preference is called for by a "good faith effort" and the failure on the part of those conducting searches to inform applicants which type of preference is in use. Regarding the latter issue, see my "Colleges Should Be Explicit About Who Will Be Considered for Jobs," *The Chronicle of Higher Education* 35, no. 30 (1989): B3, reprinted in appendix C.

3. Whether their use is appropriate in a school's admission and scholarship decisions is a different issue involving other considerations, and I shall not explore that subject in this essay.

4. See, for example, Leslie Pickering Francis, "In Defense of Affirmative Action," in *Affirmative Action and the University: A Philosophical Inquiry*, ed. Steven M. Cahn, 24–26 (Philadelphia: Temple University Press, 1993). She raises concerns about unfairness to those individuals forced by circumstances not of their own making to bear all the costs of compensation, as well as injustices to those who have been equally victimized but are not members of specified groups.

5. The terms gained currency when Justice Lewis Powell, in his pivotal opinion in the Supreme Court's 1979 *Bakke* decision, found "the attainment of a diverse student body" to be a goal that might justify the use of race in student admissions. An incisive analysis of that decision is Carl Cohen, *Naked Racial Preference* (Lanham, Md.: Madison Books, 1995), 55–80.

6. John Kekes, "The Injustice of Strong Affirmative Action," in *Affirmative Action and the University: A Philosophical Inquiry*, ed. Steven M. Cahn, 144–56 (Philadelphia: Temple University Press, 1993), 151.

7. Consider Michael Rosenfeld, *Affirmative Action and Justice: A Philosophical and Constitutional Inquiry* (New Haven, Conn.: Yale University Press, 1991), 336: "Ironically, the sooner affirmative action is allowed to complete its mission, the sooner the need for it will altogether disappear."

8. See, for example, Francis, "In Defense of Affirmative Action," 31.

9. See, for example, Richard Wasserstrom, "The University and the Case for Preferential Treatment," *American Philosophical Quarterly* 13, no. 4 (1976): 165–70.

10. See, for example, Joel J. Kupperman, "Affirmative Action: Relevant Knowledge and Relevant Ignorance," in *Affirmative Action and the University: A Philosophical Inquiry*, ed. Steven M. Cahn, 181–88 (Philadelphia: Temple University Press, 1993).

11. Consider Judith Jarvis Thomson, "Preferential Hiring," *Philosophy and Public Affairs* 2, no. 4 (1973): 368: "I do not think that as a student I learned any better, or any more, from the women who taught me than from the men, and I do not think that my own women students now learn any better or any more from me than they do from my male colleagues."

12. Celia Wolf-Devine, "Proportional Representation of Women and Minorities," in *Affirmative Action and the University: A Philosophical Inquiry*, ed. Steven M. Cahn, 223–32 (Philadelphia: Temple University Press, 1993), 230.

13. This article originally appeared in *Academe* 83, no. 1 (1997): 14.

Appendix C

1. This article originally appeared as "Colleges Should Be Explicit About Who Will Be Considered for Jobs," *The Chronicle of Higher Education* 35, no. 30 (1989): B3.

Appendix D

1. This article originally appeared in *Academe* 90, no. 1 (2004): 32–33.

Appendix E

1. This article originally appeared in *Teaching Philosophy* 27, no. 4 (2004): 321. For some years, I offered the course annually with striking results each time.

~

Suggestions for Further Reading

In the early 1990s I was general editor of a series of books published by
Rowman & Littlefield titled "Issues in Academic Ethics," with each volume
devoted to a different aspect of the subject. I list them here by title, author,
and date:

University-Business Partnerships: An Assessment
  Norman E. Bowie (1994)

Campus Rules and Moral Community: In Place of In Loco Parentis
  David A. Hoekema (1994)

A Professor's Duties: Ethical Issues in College Teaching
  Peter J. Markie (1994)

Ethics of Scientific Research
  Kristin Shrader-Frechette (1994)

Neutrality and the Academic Ethic
  Robert L. Simon (1994)

Academic Freedom and Tenure: Ethical Issues
  Richard T. De George (1997)

*Diversity and Community in the Academy: Affirmative Action in Faculty
Appointments*
  Celia Wolf-Devine (1997)

The Moral Dimensions of Academic Administration
    Rudolf H. Weingartner (1999)

Free Speech on Campus
    Martin P. Golding (2000)

Sexual Harassment as an Ethical Issue in Academic Life
    Leslie Pickering Francis (2001)

Unionization in the Academy: Visions and Reality
    Judith Wagner DeCew (2003)

Moral Leadership: Ethics and the College Presidency
    Paul J. Olscamp (2003)

Ethics and College Sports
    Peter A. French (2004)

Peer Review: A Critical Inquiry
    David Shatz (2004)

The Kindness of Strangers: Philanthropy and Higher Education
    Deni Elliott (2006)

All combine an original monograph with supplementary sources, such as philosophy articles, legal opinions, or university documents, chosen by the author to amplify the text. Together the works offer an inviting avenue to the study of academic ethics.

Index

About the Author

Steven M. Cahn is Professor of Philosophy at The City University of New York Graduate Center, where he served for nearly a decade as Provost and Vice President for Academic Affairs, then as Acting President.

He was born in Springfield, Massachusetts, in 1942, and earned his B.A. degree from Columbia College in 1963 and his Ph.D. in philosophy from Columbia University in 1966. He taught at Dartmouth College, Vassar College, New York University, the University of Rochester, and at the University of Vermont, where he chaired the Department of Philosophy.

He served as a Program Officer at the Exxon Education Foundation, as Acting Director for Humanities at The Rockefeller Foundation, and as the first Director of General Programs at the National Endowment for the Humanities. He formerly chaired the American Philosophical Association's Committee on the Teaching of Philosophy, was the Association's Delegate to the American Council of Learned Societies, and has been longtime President of The John Dewey Foundation.

Dr. Cahn is the author of nine books, including *Fate, Logic, and Time*; *The Eclipse of Excellence*; *Education and the Democratic Ideal*; *Puzzles & Perplexities: Collected Essays*, Second Edition; *God, Reason and Religion*; and *From Student to Scholar: A Candid Guide to Becoming a Professor*.

He has edited or co-edited more than thirty books, including *Classic and Contemporary Readings in the Philosophy of Education*; *Political Philosophy: The Essential Texts*, now in its second edition; *Exploring Philosophy: An Introductory Anthology*, now in its third edition; and *Ethics: History, Theory, and Contemporary Issues*, now in its fourth edition. His widely used anthology, *Classics of Western Philosophy*, is in its seventh edition.

He has been general editor of four multi-volume series: *Blackwell Philosophy Guides*, twenty-one books; *Blackwell Readings in Philosophy*, fourteen books; *Issues in Academic Ethics*, fifteen books; and *Critical Essays on the Classics*, twenty books. The latter two series are published by Rowman & Littlefield.

His numerous articles have appeared in a broad spectrum of publications, including *The Journal of Philosophy*, *The Chronicle of Higher Education*, *Shakespeare Quarterly*, *The American Journal of Medicine*, *The New Republic*, and *The New York Times*.

A collection of essays written in honor of Dr. Cahn has been published by Lexington Books. Co-edited by two of his former doctoral students, Robert B. Talisse of Vanderbilt University and Maureen Eckert of the University of Massachusetts, Dartmouth, the book is titled *A Teacher's Life: Essays for Steven M. Cahn*.